Dancing with Chihuahuas

Jeff Jenkins

A.H. STOCKWELL
PUBLISHERS SINCE 1898

S

First published in 2013
This second edition
Published in 2025 by
Jeff Jenkins
in association with
Arthur H. Stockwell
ahstockwell.com

Contents

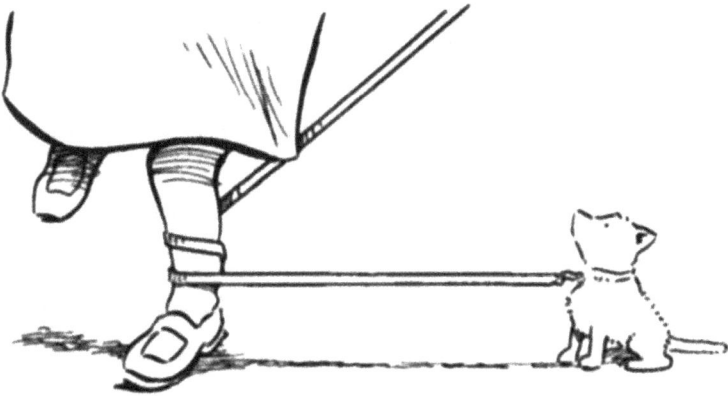

Dancing with Chihuahuas

As it says on the back cover, if you were expecting a follow-up to *Dances with Wolves*, this isn't it! It is, however, a good place to start describing all those little daily events which go unnoticed by almost everybody, unless of course that somebody happens to be me!

I know what you're thinking. You're thinking, 'Why doesn't he mind his own business?' But that is the point: I am usually trying to mind my own business when something untoward happens right in front of me. I'm sure these things happen to other people, or perhaps they just don't notice it? Either way, they do happen to me, with almost endless regularity!

Allow me to start with the title of the book and this chapter.

It was early in the morning. I couldn't tell you the exact time, but it was late enough for the sun to be up and it looked like being a lovely summer's day, but too early for any of the shops to be open. The city centre was busy with people heading for work, and children holding on till the very last minute before heading for school. So to see someone walking their dog in this melee, and not in the local park just down the road, was a little unusual.

What made it all the more unusual was the slow speed this particular very large lady was walking, with what initially appeared to be a guinea pig on a lead, although on closer inspection it turned out to be a chihuahua.

Her walking speed became slower and slower until she was almost walking in slow motion. The reason for this seemed to be that she was distracted by the numerous objects in Boots' window. Their summer sale was on and the various fifty per cent offs and BOGOFs were attracting her attention, and she had very clearly forgotten she was holding a dog lead in her left hand.

The chihuahua was obviously not interested and continued walking and facing straight ahead, but the lead now entangled itself around her left leg – once, then twice, then a third time. Once more and she was going over, no question about it, but just as the lead was about to wrap itself around for a fourth time, this time it being her right leg, she noticed, and the situation was saved.

Oh no, it doesn't end there!

Standing outside Boots on a gloriously sunny morning, a woman tied up to a chihuahua is not something you would expect to see when you wake up in the morning. Nevertheless what followed as she extricated herself from the situation was truly amazing!

Still holding the lead in her left hand and away from her body, she promptly lifted her right leg into the air and began an elaborate dance which involved her initially turning around, spinning backwards, and then pirouetting on her left leg, twice, to unravel herself.

It was very deftly done, I might add, and, believe me, she was a *very* large lady!

She had actually moved back several paces during her double pirouette; but landing back on both feet and completely unfazed, she walked past the shop window for a second time and continued on her way.

Only the two of us witnessed her dance. Her equally unfazed chihuahua, and me, watching with my mouth open!

Hello… Laura?

One cloudy but dry early spring morning found me on the 11.45 train out of London Euston on my way to Milton Keynes (no, not to see the concrete cows), and, although not a long trip, I did not expect to hear what turned out to be one of the most inane mobile-phone conversations ever.

The train wasn't full and there was a only a slight hubbub of conversation. All of a sudden, the chap on the other side of the gangway and down the carriage a couple of seats made the call.

"Hello, Laura. Yeah, Laura. Laura? It's me. I say, it's me. I'm on the train, so if I get cut off I will ring you back. I say, if I get cut off, I will ring you back. No, I said if I get cut off I will ring you back. Ring you back, yes, will ring you back. No, I'm on the train. Laura, Laura, are you there, Laura?"

We now had a pause as he looked at his, momentarily useless, mobile phone. A press of the redial button, though, soon sparked it into life again – unfortunately!

"Hello… Laura? It's me, Laura. Are you there, Laura? I'm on the train, Laura. I say, I'm on the train, Laura. Laura? If I get cut off, I will ring you back, ring you back. No, ring you back. Hello. Laura? Laura, if I get cut off…"

A slight sigh at this point obviously meant he had been cut off (or Laura had put the phone down), but he wasn't giving up that easily.

"Hello… Laura? It's me, Laura. I'm on the train, so if I get cut off I'll ring you back, will ring you back, yes. So, I'm on the train and… Oh!"

Yet again the phone cut off; yet again he phoned her back!

"Hello… Laura? Yes, I said I'd phone you back. No, I did say I'd phone you back. Anyway, I'm on the train and it's just pulling into the station so I will see you in a minute, in a minute, yes. What did you say? Oh!"

The phone had obviously cut off again and the train was indeed now pulling into the station, but there was still one last go to be had!

"Hello… Laura? Laura? Yes, I am on the train, and yes it is pulling into the station. Laura? Yes, I am on the train! Yes, it is pulling into the station! See you in a minute, yes. Yes, see you in a minute. Hello… Laura? Laura?"

With that he stood up, slipped the mobile phone into his inside jacket pocket, took his briefcase down from the luggage rack and arrived at the automatic doors just as the train came to a stop. Where the train had come to rest at the platform there was a lady waiting for him. Can you guess who it was?

Wotsit Look Like?

An almost weekly visit to the local Co-op is always an experience. An experience at which I seem to be getting quicker and quicker, as I think I have found a way to dodge around the customers (and staff) who seem to constantly dither in the aisles. There is always someone standing in the exact spot when I want a loaf of bread, or blocking the cold cabinets when I want a bag of rippidy-chippidies (that's crinkle-cut oven chips to the uninitiated).

I have a quick shufti round the store before picking anything up to see where everybody is, then go round in the order of least number of people at each place. The boffin who first said "Man is a hunter-gatherer" was spot on!

However, this particular day the wheels fell off! An elderly lady, complete with walking stick, was everywhere I went. How she managed to do it I will never know. I picked up apples, there she was. Carrots, there she was. Semi-skimmed milk, there she was. Even when I made a beeline for a four-pack of toilet rolls with fifty per cent off, there she was!

So of course when I finally arrived at the till, guess what?

Yep, there she was, standing right in front of me and unloading all the contents of her basket onto the conveyor belt.

She was about halfway through the unloading when something suddenly occurred to her.

"Oh, where's my walking stick!" she exclaimed, before looking around at the harassed throng standing behind her in the queue. "Has anybody seen it?" she added.

But no answer came. In fact no more than a bottom-lip-curling shoulder-shrugging response came from staff and customers alike.

The storeroom is accessed by a keypad entry system, and as a member of staff came out the supervisor shouted across, "Have you seen this lady's walking stick?"

The staff member prevented the door from closing with her right leg, while peering first left and then right, and then left again behind the heavy iron door. It was probably less than ten seconds, but seemed like hours as we held our breath, and the tension mounted.

Finally, came her reply: "Wotsit look like?"

I smiled to myself. I'm sorry, folks, but I just couldn't resist saying it out loud: "Er, a walking stick!"

"Yeah, wotsit look like?" replied the member of staff directly to me. Would you believe I was stuck for an answer! I mean, just how many walking sticks do they have behind the storeroom door of the Co-op?

Suddenly a disembodied voice came from aisle two: "Found it!" it cried.

A male member of staff had found it 'down the other end' and now appeared carrying triumphantly the misplaced stick like an Olympic torch.

Panic over. The elderly lady had her stick back, normality reigned once more and the world started turning again.

Water, Water, Everywhere...

I've noticed whenever you have two retired couples sitting together in a restaurant there is always a case of one-upmanship and a general beat-your-neighbour competition going on between the two men of the party.

One particular earwigged conversation involved this chap who clearly had spent some time on a ship, as he seemed to know everything there was to know. Between you and me, though, I think the only ships he had been on were day trips to see the *Mary Rose*, along with a poke round HMS *Victory*! He clearly wanted an audience so he proceeded to speak louder – and louder!

"Because ships today they're all blah-blah fitted with this, that and the other blah-blah, so they will never encounter an iceberg in the North Atlantic. And, I would like to add, they've not just got a thingummy wotsit, but most have a blah-blah thingummy wotsit with a blah-blah sprocket fitted, meaning the *Titanic* could never ever happen again!"

Pause for effect, quick look around to see who might be listening, go again.

"Well, when I say never, I suppose it could, couldn't it? Ships do still hit things, and still sink even with a blah-blah thingummy wotsit, and whether there's a sprocket fitted to it or not, blah-blah."

Throughout the whole of this diatribe his thoroughly bored wife kept eating her prawn cocktail, although her head was going further and further down towards it. I swear at one point her nose brushed the edge of the bed of lettuce her dozen prawns were resting on.

The other couple sat equally bored, or mesmerized, it was hard to tell which, but he wasn't going to stop now he was in full flow.

But then disaster struck! So as to emphasise his next point, he gesticulated wildly with his right hand, catching the almost full water jug the waitress had only placed on the table about thirty seconds earlier.

Everywhere was soaked. The table was soaked, the carpet was soaked, his wife was soaked. His garlic-mushroom starter was soaked to the extent that they washed off the plate and cascaded onto the soaked carpet. His trousers and shirt were soaked, and even the radiator next to him hissed slightly as water dripped off the far edge of the table and onto it.

Nobody spoke. Nobody needed to. Waitresses arrived from all quarters to start mopping (or bailing, depending on how you look at it), and the whole ensemble had to move to another table to continue their meal – in absolute silence, I might add. Not a word was spoken between any of them.

There was quite literally water everywhere you looked. A bit like the *Titanic* really!

Do I Look Like a Walking A–Z?

Well, obviously I don't have the blue and red lettering of an A–Z guide stamped on my forehead, so why am I asking this question I hear you ask? I'll tell you.

Because you cannot possibly believe the incredibly inconceivable amount of times I have been stopped and asked for directions!

Cars from absolutely out of nowhere have pulled up next to me while I've been walking along the street minding my own business, brakes slammed on and with a protesting loud squeak from the tyres as they skid to a halt.

The window on the passenger side whizzes down and the wife flops back into her seat, having previously been thrown forward as a result of the sudden stop. She has her finger on the map and usually opens her mouth to say something, but nothing ever comes out. It's always the driver (her husband, I'm guessing) that speaks first.

"'Ere, mate, are we goin' the right way for the seafront?" (Not bad when you consider we're four miles inland.)

"Er, no, you'll have to go all the way round the next roundabout, come back this way and then it's four miles to…" I don't have a chance of finishing the sentence.

"Cheers mate!" says the driver. Window whirrs back up, and you always hear a "Told ya!" to the wife just as it winds back into position.

I can honestly say I have never gone two weeks in the last thirty years without at least one directional request. I think it began when I used to have the occasional wander around B&Q in my lunch break.

A large superstore was opposite the office where I worked, and while looking around I would often be stopped and asked, "'Ere, mate, do you know where they keep the two-inch washers?"

I've even had "'Ere, mate, does this kill greenfly as well as aphids?" whilst having an anti-bug mixture waved under my nose.

People have said to me it was probably because I was wearing a suit at the time, and the punters perhaps assumed I was the area manager. Although taking the jacket off didn't help, as only in a shirt and tie the requests still came thick and fast.

"'Ere, mate, when's the best time for planting winter cabbages?" says a bloke with a packet of seeds in one hand and a four-pronged garden fork in the other.

The worst of it is, instead of saying, "I can't help" or, "Sorry, but I don't work here," I start to make it up: "The second week of September is usually best, I always think."

And off goes our gardener very happy with a "Cheers, mate!" as he disappears into the distance.

Time moved on and I changed workplaces, but it didn't stop. Where I worked it was a short walk into town and one day standing outside W. H. Smith I had a request.

"'Ere, mate, where's Smiffs?" asked a suited-and-booted gent.

"Er, here!" I replied in semi-disbelief at the request while at the same time pointing over both shoulders with both index fingers.

"Oh, cheers, mate!" came back the reply.

And it gets worse inside. Having found the magazine I was looking for and reached the contemplation stage as to whether I was buying it or not, there would invariably be a tap on my arm and/or a tug on my sleeve.

"Excuse me. Do you know where I can find *Canal Boat Holidays?*" The request came from a small round woman who looked as though she had been in 'Smiffs' for days searching for this one magazine.

On this occasion I decided to help her. I put my magazine back on the shelf and joined in the search, the whole time being told the story of her trip to the Kennet and Avon last year and how much she had enjoyed it, even though the bread fell into the water by accident on the second day and the ducks ate it.

That particular story is an exception as she did actually use the words 'Excuse me' and not ''Ere, mate!' In fact, ''Ere, mate!' is used almost without exception every time to prefix a directional request.

"'Ere, mate, where's the council offices?" came a request only the other day when a huge Bentley drew up next to where I was walking.

"Oh, you're miles out," I replied, and decided to give him directions – through the ring road and the one-way system. That'll teach him to get lost.

I wouldn't mind, but we have satnavs now and it's not made a difference to me. The requests haven't slowed down any. In fact, I've noticed I'm being singled out more and more. There's people behind and in front of me when I'm walking, but the drivers never stop and ask them, only me!

I was on a sightseeing trip to London once. (Don't even get me started on how many times I've been asked on the Underground, "'Ere, mate, do you know the way to..?") This chap, probably in his mid-seventies, suddenly touched my arm.

"'Ere, mate, have you seen my wife? I've lost her, see."

I had absolutely no idea who he was, let alone who his wife could be. Surely the look of disbelief on my face answered his question – but no, clearly not.

"Is that her?" I replied, whilst gesticulating towards a girl of perhaps seventeen wearing shorts and a boob tube.

"No," he replied in all seriousness before quickly adding, "Oh, it's all right, I've seen her." And he disappeared into the crowd, but not before saying, "Thanks for your help!" equally seriously.

I just don't understand it. Why me? I can guarantee I will have been asked directions, and had an "Ere mate!' on at least a dozen occasions between me writing this chapter and you reading it!

Go On, Ask Me Whodunnit

A chilly end of June gave way to a warm July and the decision was taken to have a day in London before the kids broke up from school and the tourists descended on the place. The day out in London was not a new idea; it was something that me and my girlfriend did on a regular basis, usually taking in a landmark such as St Paul's Cathedral or the London Eye. Even 'Duck Tours' has been part of the day-trip experience. These day trips usually started with a visit to Leicester Square and the ticket booths to see if there were any tickets going spare for one of the musicals in the West End, and then ended with an early dinner, a dance in the aisles and the last train home.

This particular day was the same as any other day trip: we hadn't planned on anywhere to visit or on any particular show, so it was a make-it-up-as-you-go-along kind of day. The thing was, it was hot. Very hot. On the train it wasn't even half past ten and it was hot. Gasping for air at London Victoria was hopeless because it was even hotter there too.

The day went ahead, though, as planned, and before we

knew it we were standing waiting to catch the Tube to Leicester Square. The instant sirocco to be had when the train rushed up to the platform was the only relief from the oppressive heat.

Has anyone out there ever decided to run up the steps at Leicester Square Tube Station? Well, today for some mad reason we decided to do it. For those of you that don't know, there is a dark staircase at Leicester Square Tube Station that leads from the bottom all the way up and out onto the street at the top, no escalators involved. About five minutes after you've thought it can't be any further, you still find yourself climbing. With knees and calf muscles aching, you burst out onto the street gasping for air.

After a semi-asthma attack all round, composure was regained and we set off for the booths and two tickets to something. Joining the queue for one booth, I suddenly had an inspiration.

"How about going to see *The Mousetrap*?" I spluttered. "I mean, I know it's not a musical but it would make a change going to see a play, wouldn't it?"

Arriving at the front of the queue we startled the woman on the counter with our request.

"Oh no," she said haughtily, "we don't sell them. You will have to go to the theatre direct and buy them there."

Having obtained directions to the theatre, upon arrival we found the place closed. Actually it looked more like closed down, but the sign on the door said that they opened at twelve o'clock and it was five to at the time. Sure enough, just after twelve a tweedily dressed lady unlocked the door and was slightly taken aback to see two potential punters standing on the pavement. Ushering us inside, she even gave a quick look up and down the street to see either if anyone had noticed her opening the door, or if we were the start of the rush. Having purchased two tickets from her for that evening's performance, we set off on the next objective of visiting somewhere or something.

It was by now very, very hot. Mad dogs and Englishmen sprang to mind as we wandered back, trying to decide what to do and where to go. Nowhere particular sprang to mind, so it was decided that a drink and some nibbles were called for to lubricate the little grey cells. Stopping off at a small twenty-four-hour supermarket, we decided on buying a four-pack of lager, a sandwich each, crisps and salted peanuts and wandered up to Soho Square for a sit in the sun while contemplating what to do next.

It was now what you might call boiling. Finding a patch of grass we sat down and, to put it mildly, the first can of lager didn't touch the sides! However, whilst munching the crisps, we were aware that all around us something wasn't quite right. There were lots of groups of people doing the same as us and sitting on the grass either eating or drinking or both. The thing was all the groups were of the same sex. We were obviously in a park surrounded by – how can I put this? – 'Beautiful People', and clearly me and my girlfriend were drawing curiosity glances. We didn't care, though. It was hot and we opened the next two cans. They didn't last much longer than the first two.

"I've got something else too," she said suddenly, and from out of her knapsack, which was posing as a handbag, she produced a bottle of sparkling wine and two plastic champagne flutes.

"Now you tell me! Well, don't stand on ceremony," I said while waving my empty flute from side to side.

She fiddled with the silver paper and in one very deft movement loosened and took off the wire holding the plastic cork. Her thumbs went from red to white as she pushed at the cork, tried unscrewing it and tried pulling at it, but it was finally the double thumb push that eased it from the bottle. Only thing was, though, the gradual shaking of the bottle in the efforts to loosen it had churned the contents inside of it up somewhat. The cork flew out of the bottle with a resounding pop and went like an Exocet missile across Soho Square. Can you guess where it landed? A group of several 'Nice Boys' sitting together and minding their own business were suddenly rudely interrupted as a plastic cork landed right in the middle of their picnic. To be honest, I was more concerned about the loss of about a quarter of the wine, which had followed the cork out of the bottle and in the process had coated and unsalted our peanuts, than whether any of them were suffering with head wounds.

After a sit and lie in the sun it was time to move on, and we wandered off in the direction of the nearest Kentucky Fried Chicken. However, while wandering, we walked past a bar, standing outside of which was this huge geezer. In his hand he held a glass and was drinking from it. The glass contained a cocktail, and while no comment was passed regarding the actual size of this bloke, which was about eight feet in all directions, it was as to the scrumminess of the cocktail he was holding. With coos of "Cor, that looks nice!" and "Shall we pop in and have one?" we soon found ourselves standing at the bar. Her ladyship had to use the loo, but when she came back she found me with a look of shock on my face with my hand outstretched and a pound coin nestling in my palm.

"Have you just found that?" she queried.

"No, it's my change," I stammered.

"From a tenner!" she exclaimed.

"Er, no, from a twenty. They're £9.50 each!"

Funnily enough, we only had the one each and made them last. Couldn't tell you what was in it, but it was pretty potent and tasted superb on top of lager and sparkling wine.

From the cocktail bar a KFC was found, and two pieces of chicken 'n' chips twice were ordered and scoffed. The time was ticking on, so we headed off in the direction of the theatre.

Arriving too early, we decided to pop into a pub. It looked quiet on the outside, but was absolutely packed on the inside with theatregoers. It seemed everybody else had the same idea.

Deciding on a glass of wine each, the barman kindly informed us that "For a coupla quid, ya can get the rest of the bottle free."

What a helpful chap! How could we resist such an offer?

Ten minutes to curtain-up, we staggered across the road and into the theatre. We showed the usher our tickets and, although he explained where they were, it was not without a little difficulty that we found our seats.

Did you know that Agatha Christie's *The Mousetrap* has been running on the stage longer than most people in this country have been alive? Well, that was part of the attraction of wanting to see it. It has never been done as a film or television production and can't be until it comes off the stage, and that doesn't look like being anytime soon.

So why don't I tell you all about it. Erm, methinks that's going to be a bit tricky. Towards the end of the first half the lady next door but one to me in the row on my left-hand side poked me in the arm. Pointing a bony finger at my girlfriend, on the other side of me, she stated quite snootily that "She's snoring!" She was too, although to be honest I hadn't noticed her passed out on my shoulder.

"Probably too much… sun," I pleaded for her in her defence.

I don't think the woman bought it, though, although I don't know why not because I'm sure it was the sun that was starting to affect my eyeballs and powers of concentration too! Between you and me I think it might have been the rest of the 'free' wine in the bottle, although a cocktail with several spirits in it may be partly to blame; and we hardly had any lager, so it definitely wasn't that(!).

Needless to say, my memories of watching *The Mousetrap* consist of seeing two couples dressed in tweeds in a country house and, er, well, er, that's about it.

A lovely day out was had by all. Some drinks – OK, quite a few actually – a takeaway, a mooch around London and ending with seeing the longest-running play of all time. But go on then, ask me whodunnit? Blessed if I could tell you. Don't worry, Agatha, the secret is well and truly safe with me.

A WEIRD AND WONDERFUL HISTORY OF JOB INTERVIEWS PART ONE

The Great Tower Bridge Road Job Interview

The advert in the paper was short, to say the least. All it seemed I had to do was phone the number and I would get an interview. It didn't say what the job was, only that it was based in Tower Bridge Road in London.

"What a great place to work!" I actually said out loud.

I phoned the number, and a young lady with a squeaky voice answered.

"Yes, that's right," she said. "Come along next Tuesday. Does eleven o'clock suit you?" The question came to an end with a high-pitched squeak.

I told her it did and that I would be there.

I had been made redundant from my last job, and, apart from a few fixed-term temporary posts, I hadn't had a full-time job since, so this sounded hopeful. And of course I was getting on in years – well in job terms anyway, as I was fast approaching thirty! Very fast, in fact, as it was only a month away!

I hadn't been to the Tower of London since a school trip years ago, so emerging from Tower Hill Underground Station with the Tower right in front of me on a glorious summer morning I was reminded just how good it looked. Deciding to take a walk around the perimeter and then over Tower Bridge itself, I managed to lose all track of time, and, along with thousands of tourists stopping right in front of me every few moments to take photographs, I was seriously going to have to get a wiggle on to get to my eleven-o'clock interview.

Finally I made it, and on time, to where the address was, except it wasn't! Let me explain. The address I had written down was something like 634, but between 632 and 636 there was, well, nothing! The only thing breaking the symmetry was a recessed black steel door which didn't look like it had been opened since the war. The huge pile of dog ends, the squished compacted chewing gum and the suspicious stains up the walls brought me to that conclusion.

'This can't be it,' I thought while pulling on the sticky black handle of the door. It was, though – proved by the fact that the door opened.

I was now standing at the bottom of a very dimly lit staircase, which had been carpeted with a red floral carpet probably about fifty years ago! Thinking this was not one of my best ideas, and wondering whether I should leave now, I was brought to my senses by the clanging of the metal door behind me.

Walking up the stairs was a journey in itself, as on almost every stair the carpet slipped from under my feet. To say the place was a deathtrap may be a slight understatement!

Six flights of treacherous stairs later I reached the top. Other than the stained and peeling-away-from-the-skirting-board carpet, to my left was an open door, and nothing else – not that you could see very much else, due to the dimly lit bulb hanging precariously down from the yellowing plastered ceiling.

I walked through the open door and immediately to my

right was a table, sat at which were two people, a greying gent in his late fifties and a woman with a blonde bob haircut, probably about my age, seated on his left.

I addressed them both. "Hello. I've come for an interview at, erm, eleven o'clock," I stammered.

"Oh yes," she replied. "What's the name?"

"Jeff Jenkins," I replied.

What happened next was slightly odd. Instead of ticking me off her list, she wrote my name down at the top of a piece of paper.

I now stood there in silence while the gent started shuffling several sheets of paper about. Having finally got them into an order he was satisfied with, he handed them to the woman, who from out of nowhere produced a clipboard and attached them all to it.

"If you'd just like to fill these out for me, please," she said, and handed me the whole ensemble. It was seven sheets of questions.

Before I could speak, she had handed me a small blue pen.

"Is there somewhere I can sit down?" I asked, with my patience now slipping.

"There's a seat behind you," she replied, half looking and half gesticulating with her left hand at the same time.

This was the first time I had turned around.

Behind me, sitting in complete silence, were about twenty people, all with their legs crossed, all balancing a clipboard on one leg and filling out their multi-questionnaires with a small blue pen.

The seat nearest to me was empty, so I sat myself down on it and assumed the same position.

I scanned the questions on the sheets. There was nothing on there they didn't want to know. I wrote my name and date of birth at the top and skimmed the rest of the questions on the first page. Before filling them out I shot a quick glance at the rest of the people around me. I'm pretty certain not one of them was eighteen!

'What am I doing here?' crossed my mind, not for the first time.

I skimmed the questions again, not just on the top page but the other six pages as well. There was no clue whatsoever about exactly what I was applying for!

The next part all happened in real time.

I flopped the pages back down onto the clipboard, carefully removed the top one with my name and date of birth on it, stood up, handed the clipboard with the remaining pages and pen back to the woman and said "Thank you!" Then I walked out the door, turned right, and six flights of treacherous stairs later I reached the bottom. The recessed black steel door had a black sticky handle on this side of it as well! Opening it, I was now back outside.

I was now standing back on Tower Bridge Road. No interview, no nearer finding a job, but to this day I still wonder what the job might have been.

Still, it was a lovely day and it seemed such a shame to waste it. I walked back over Tower Bridge and spent a really fabulous afternoon in the Tower of London, although I must admit I did look a little out of place dressed in a pinstriped suit!

Doggy-Bagging Ya Naan

Thursday is curry night at Wetherspoons! I'm guessing this hasn't always been the case and I'm also sure at some point in the future it won't be again, but for the present it is.

In every instance where I have partaken of one of their curries, nothing particularly untoward has happened, except on this one notable occasion.

A friend and myself had a long-standing plan for a curry night, and the reasonably priced meal, together with a free drink, at Wetherspoons appealed.

We didn't actually meet until 7.15, and I can assure you our curries were eaten and washed down by 8.30, although more liquid refreshment was required!

"My shout!" cried Steve as he grabbed my empty glass and headed over to the bar for replenishments.

With him gone, my eyeline was no longer interrupted, and into my view came two quite elderly gents who were sitting talking several feet away.

After a few moments, the waitress appeared. They too were

embarking on 'curries all round' and she placed the meals in front of them.

Their conversation now came to an abrupt halt as they embarked on demolishing their curries. They wolfed the lot – curries and poppadoms, even down to the last grain of rice on their plates. There was nothing left, except, for reasons we will perhaps never know, they did not touch one single crumb of their naan bread!

The conversation now started up again, but seemed to be in hushed tones. The one who slightly had his back to me now began ferreting for something under the table, while the one facing me kept a lookout for the returning waitress.

From under the table appeared a small brown bag and the one with his back to me had a quick look around as he secretly slipped the untouched naan bread from his plate and into the bag. The next stage of the operation involved the one facing me exchanging their plates. They both had another quick look around and the one with his back to me carried out the smuggling operation for a second time.

With the four pieces of naan bread successfully snaffled, the bag disappeared below the table. Another quick look around was made to see who had noticed their smuggling operation. No one of course had, other than yours truly.

Steve had by now worked out that his last five minutes of conversation had been lost, as he noticed by the look of curiosity on my face that I hadn't been listening.

"You all right, mate?" he asked quizzically.

"Yeah, yeah, fine," I distractedly replied.

The waitress returned and cleared away the elderly gents' empty plates and dishes. As soon as she had gone, they drained their glasses, stood up and put their coats on. The naan smuggler clearly did not have a pocket large enough to take the brown bag crammed with four pieces of naan bread, so, with yet another look around, he held it underneath his coat at the position where his inside pocket would be.

The two of them couldn't get out of there fast enough.

It does make you wonder, though. Perhaps they had a buyer waiting just outside. Perhaps they were just out to corner the naan-bread market. Or is there a secret dark society of naan-bread smugglers out there? I do so hope there is!

Can You Lend Us a Tenner?

(Overheard Office Conversation, Just Before Lunchtime)

First Lady: "Can you lend us a tenner?"

Second Lady: "No, I don't use them, sorry."

First Lady: "No I meant a £10 note. I wasn't asking for a feminine hygiene product!"

Misunderstanding sorted, she happily skipped off with her £10 note.

The lady that didn't use them then stated, "Do you know, she's the kind of person who wouldn't throw a drowning man a lifebelt. She would get the person standing next to her to throw the drowning man a lifebelt, and then spend the next ten minutes telling them how they could have thrown it better!"

The Flying Sausage

The day dawned a little misty and hazy in the fair city of Lichfield. The weather forecast suggested it would be warm and sunny, so there was no rush with breakfast – take your time, let the sun come out and enjoy the day sightseeing.

To be honest, breakfast wasn't that special. It was one of those serve-yourself buffet-style, eat-as-many-fried-eggs-as-you-like types of breakfast, where the bacon is usually cremated and the scrambled egg is always sloppy.

Actually what I had to eat was OK-ish with no complaints from me (for a change) – or from anyone else, come to that. However, I was just coming to the end of my fourth slice of toast when something on the table adjacent to mine caught my eye.

A lady in maybe her late seventies was making a strange up-and-down movement with her right arm. The flapping sleeve of her cardigan was not helping with my general nosiness, so I moved my chair slightly to get a better view! Just what was she doing?

Her right arm was now vertical from the elbow downwards, and in her hand she was holding a knife with which she was clearly stabbing at something, and not succeeding. After a minute or so she stopped and I could see it was a sausage, and a very cremated one too – in fact, one of three she had on her plate, all equally cremated.

She decided on a new plan of attack.

During the stabbing she had held a fork in her left hand. This she now abandoned, and instead held the sausage down on her plate with her left hand while her right hand took up the knife again. She sawed away at this sausage like there was no tomorrow. The table creaked and protested loudly from all its four legs, her tea cup clinked up and down on its saucer, and the sleeve of her cardigan flapped back and forth like a flag in a hurricane, but still she hardly made an impression on the skin of this sausage.

This was clearly not going to work either, so after a moment's hesitation she went back to Plan A, but with a slight change. This time she used her left hand to hold the sausage and not the fork, and stab down with the knife in her right hand. It was at this point the sausage decided it had had enough, and the inevitable happened.

The downward pressure fired the sausage through the air like an Exocet missile. It would have travelled for miles – halfway across Staffordshire probably – but fortunately it slammed into the pillar only a few feet from her. It left a nice greasy mark halfway up the freshly magnolia-painted pillar and flew upwards briefly before falling back to earth and proceeding to roll right under her chair.

She wasn't done yet, though. Unable to reach it from sitting down, she stood up, ferreted around under her chair for a minute or two and retrieved the sausage. All attempts to cut it now abandoned, she instead just put it in her mouth and chomped down on it with absolutely no problem at all, which begs the question, why didn't she do that in the first place?

The remaining two sausages she ate the same way, upon the completion of which she stopped the waitress (struggling under the weight of several large dirty plates) in her tracks, and asked her if she could have some more toast.

At this point, with the sun coming out and my own breakfast finished, I decided to leave her to it!

The Muffin Snatchers

An evening out once necessitated an overnight stay in a Premier Inn. As the previous evening had largely been a liquid affair, the do-it-yourself breakfast was eagerly anticipated!

A good fry-up was had by all, but I delayed making my toast until I had my bacon 'n' eggs, so that it was nice and hot when it came out fresh from the toasting machine. So, with breakfast eaten, and clutching two slices of white bread from the bread basket, I placed them both carefully onto the revolving grill.

At almost exactly the same moment a man and a woman appeared. They were definitely not staff; in fact, they were probably just two other paying guests, and I wouldn't have noticed them at all if she hadn't clipped my elbow as she walked past, momentarily causing me to lose my balance (not that it takes much).

The only item they were carrying was a small brown carrier bag, and they headed past me and over to the bread basket, by the side of which was a smaller box containing at least a dozen muffins for toasting purposes.

While the woman held the bag open, the man lowered each muffin one by one carefully into the bag, and didn't stop until the box was empty and the carrier bag was bulging – so much so that the last muffin had to be literally squeezed in!

As you can imagine, with my general curiosity and nosiness, I was intrigued by this spectacle of brazen muffin snatching, which was made worse when I overheard the woman say, "I don't know what they are, but they look nice anyway!"

The man didn't reply, and without looking up just carried on filling the bag.

With the bag full, they came back towards me and headed back in the direction they had come from, with the woman clipping my elbow and momentarily causing me to lose my balance for a second time (see, I told you it didn't take much).

At almost the same moment, my toast plopped into the tray underneath the toasting machine. Once retrieved, and clutching several small butters, I headed back to my table. I hadn't been away for five minutes!

Definitely a very strange thing to happen while watching your bread toasting. Here's a thought for you all, though: do you think they could be a branch of the previously aforementioned secret dark society of naan-bread smugglers?

The Mysterious Case of the Incredible Shrinking Ma

I'm losing my mother! No, no, I don't mean to some dreadful incurable disease or even to a hooded group of ne'er-do-wells who are going to kidnap her and hold her to ransom; I mean, I'm losing her.

Yes, I know you can define losing in lots of ways, but this way isn't like having to find a supervisor in Debenhams and trying to explain to her that the last time you saw your mother was in ladies' underwear.

"But, sir, what other underwear would she be wearing?"

No, it's because my mother is slowly disappearing – downwards!

When I was knee high to, well, just about everybody my mother was the one whom I didn't have to shout loudest at as she was only just over five feet tall (in old money, that is) and therefore no more than a tug of the skirt was enough to attract her attention. No, of *her* skirt; what would a five-year-old boy be doing in a skirt?

And as I got older everybody said to me in a rather threatening manner, "Oh, you're gonna be over six foot, like your dad."

Somehow, I always knew I wasn't going to be, and had this morbid fascination as a kid that I was going to grow up to be a dwarf (isn't that called an oxymoron?); and sure enough I was right – well, not exactly right as I stopped growing at (still in old money) five foot seven. To me, though, it has always been a convenient height as I found that I didn't have to stoop down too far to cuddle young ladies, and when it came to buying 'stuff off the peg' everything fitted. Standing at a football match was a problem, though, because if I stood at the back I couldn't see anything and if I stood at the front I was invariably crushed against the advertising hoarding.

Being this tall, though, meant that I could speak to my mother all through my twenties and thirties; but since reaching the big four-o I'm finding that I'm having to speak louder because she can't hear me. I was of the opinion that she was going a bit Mutt and Jeff – but no, it's because she's getting further away – downwards!

Now, her mother lived until her early nineties and she went in the same direction, although I don't think she was ever five foot to begin with.

But my mother was, and to be honest I was getting fed up with the constant calls from her of "You're going to have to measure me, cos I swear I'm shrinking."

So when for the umpteenth time she said it, a quick root around in the shed with the torch for the tape measure preceded the moment of grand measuring. It was one of those days when you wake up thinking the day ahead will just be a normal down-to-earth, run-of-the-mill kinda day. At no point would you think that by the end of it you'll be standing your mother up against a wall as if she is about to face a firing squad for high treason and measuring her.

I'm sorry, but I have to ask you this. Is there anyone out there who has tried to keep their mother standing still, upright, and tried to measure her at the same time? Well, if you have then you have my permission to skip this bit. OK then, has anyone out there ever been shark fishing, caught one and landed it into a thirty-foot boat and then tried to keep it in the said boat? You have? Well, now you know where I'm coming from, because that's exactly what it was like. She fidgeted her way through this measuring like she had St Vitus's dance, and every time I managed to get her head still, so the rest of her moved in a swaying motion reminiscent of someone sitting on a bus or a train listening to an iPod. But somehow we got there, and a wonky pencil mark now appeared on the wall in the kitchen.

"Hold that there," I said in an I'm-starting-to-lose-my-patience-here attitude, as I gave her the end of the tape measure. I whizzed down the wall (not literally) and stopped at the bottom, whereupon she moved her feet and promptly stood on my left hand. Luckily, though, she was wearing carpet slippers so finger splints weren't required.

"It looks to me like fifty-eight and a half inches," I said, yelling up from what felt like the bottom of a well.

That did it. "See – I told you. Fifty-eight inches (the half got knocked off or she rounded it down, one or the other)! That's four feet ten inches [as if to confirm it]. I've lost two inches!" she exclaimed in an authoritative voice, which I think was directed purely at me in a 'well, don't just stand there, round up a posse and go find it' kind of voice.

A quick look round the kitchen and I concluded that there was no sign of it and I reported back: "I'm sorry – it's gone.

Someone or something has had your two inches." I was trying to make light of the situation, but it made no difference.

"Well, no wonder that skirt no longer fits" came back the reply.

Feeling that I couldn't take this any further, I slinked out of the kitchen to the relative safety of the lounge and put the telly on, in the hope that that would be an end to it once and for all – and it was, for now.

Barely a month had passed and we came full circle.

"You are going to have to measure me again – I'm shrinking" came the outburst right in the middle of *Emmerdale*.

"What, again, and right now?" I asked.

I managed to stall it that night, but not for long. Within a week we were at the kitchen wall again re-enacting the same palaver as before.

"Fifty-eight inches," I yelled.

"Oh, same as last time, then" came back the reply.

"No, you've lost half an inch – it was fifty-eight and a half before."

"See, see – I told you I was shrinking!" she shrieked.

Regular measurings have now become a part of the staple diet of our household over the last couple of years. At the last count we were down to fifty-six inches – or four foot eight inches, to put it another way, which I don't actually think helps. Me, I'm just grateful to be sixty-seven inches, and at least it means when it comes to cuddling my ma she can fit neatly under my arm. Please don't tell her that for Gawd's sake, else she'll have you round with the measuring tape just to prove that I must be doing it wrong. No, we mustn't have her upset because, well, after all, she is still my mum – what there is still left of her!

OK, Shakespeare; OK, Byron, OK, OK, OK!

The following conversation was overheard while on a bus. Well, when I say overheard, it was actually only half a conversation as I could only hear the chap at this end on his mobile phone.

To get the full effect of this conversation, you need to pause for approximately three seconds after each full stop. Are you ready? Here we go!

"Hello. Yeah. Yeah. OK. OK. OK. OK. Yeah. OK. OK. Yeah. Bye. Yeah. OK. Yeah. Bye."

And with that, he hung up and put the phone back inside his trouser pocket.

Two questions.

Is this really why the mobile phone was invented?

Is this the language of Shakespeare, Byron, Shelley and Keats?

Er, no to both questions!

Coming to the Boil with the Local Paper

A long-since defunct local newspaper once advertised for an office assistant. It looked and sounded perfect, so I duly sent them my CV.

Within three days, I received a letter in the post requesting I attend an interview the following Thursday. So far so good! However...

On the Monday morning I noticed a slight reddening and swelling on the left-hand side of my nose and dismissed it at first, but as the day wore on it began to swell a little bit more. By the evening it began to look quite big and was now starting to hurt, but I didn't do much about it. Well, as a bloke, I wouldn't, would I!

Let's skip Tuesday and go straight to Wednesday, because by now it was huge – about the size of a large pea – and, I have to say, boy did it hurt!

Thursday morning came and I had an interview to go to. The growth on the side of my nose was now about the size of a Malteser, and the colours of a Rhubarb 'n' Custard! My left eye was half closed and I could no longer close my mouth on the left side as it was pulling the skin up on my cheek. There seemed to be a strange kind of whistling sound in my left ear as well!

I put my best suit on and made my way to the bus stop. It was a twenty-five-minute bus ride followed by a fifteen-minute walk to the newspaper offices, and every second of the journey was absolute agony.

I have to be honest, I don't remember much more. I do remember, though, that it was a one-on-one interview, and I will never forget the strange look he gave me the moment I walked in the room!

I answered all his questions, although I don't know how. I could barely move my mouth – just what must I have looked like from the other side of his desk?

Needless to say, I didn't get the job. I was certainly qualified enough to do it, so I'm guessing it was something else that put him off!

The journey home was even more agonising. Looking back, I can laugh about it now, but I couldn't then – in fact, I couldn't even move my face!

The whole sorry tale came to an end on the Friday afternoon when the left side of my face literally exploded, but by then of course it was too late.

How Much Is That Doggie in the Window?

Lunchtime in any city centre is always busy; and combined with the city's market day and half-term week, you can almost guarantee a first-day-of-Harrod's-sale pushandshove.com scenario.

This particular city has its weekly market on a Wednesday and by half-twelve the world and his wife (and all their kids, come to that) were out on the street. The sun was shining, which of course always brings the populous at large out anyway; the shops were all busy and, naturally, so too was the market.

And then there were the buskers!

Throughout the length of the High Street there is always at least one busker, but with so many people out and about this particular Wednesday there were four!

Now, I like a good busker, though that is usually the problem – find a good one! Well, on this day they had one. Talk about dressed for the part! A real old rocker, complete with red-and-white spotted bandana, grey goatee beard, studded leather jacket and a never-seen-a-washing-machine-in-their-life pair of jeans.

When I walked past he was belting out Bruce Springsteen's 'Born in the USA', and while in the downstairs of a nearby department store I heard Meat Loaf's 'Bat Out of Hell'. He had quite a crowd gathered in front of him, and his deliberately left-open guitar case contained a fair smattering of coins. There was even a £5 note in there as well.

As I came out he had progressed to Bon Jovi's 'Living on a Prayer', and as I walked further down the High Street I could still hear him, this time singing 'Paranoid' by Black Sabbath. However, ten minutes later and I was on my way back up the High Street, shopping all done. It was then the myth was well and truly shattered.

Still dressed the same, but with the original crowd all gone, and replaced with several children of primary-school age with their mothers and pushchairs, he had embarked on his next song – 'How Much Is That Doggie in the Window?'!

It took me a minute or two to work out what he was actually singing as it was being sung with the same rasping voice, and so far out of tune you wouldn't believe. The kids were mesmerised! Even more so when he did the 'woof-woof' after the line, 'The one with the waggly tail'! Me, I just kept on walking.

Cos They Like a Bit of Tom Jones
Round Here, You Know

"No, I've never been either."

My girlfriend and I were discussing one cold, blowy January night which places and where we most fancied spending long weekends at various times in the forthcoming year. Although both well travelled, having been to the States and Australia and the Far East, we had never been to Wales, hence my reply when she suggested it.

"I've only ever seen South Wales on a clear day from North Devon," I added.

So after much thumbing through calendars and diaries we decided on Easter being a good time. Easter was early this particular year, so all the daffodils would still be out. You can't get more Welsh than that, can you?

A nice little B&B found from a *Cosy Weekends Are Us* brochure, in a village a few miles outside of Tenby, was soon booked and gave us something to look forward to as the dark cold days of winter gave way to the first snowdroppy days of spring.

Before we knew it, Maundy Thursday had arrived, and having taken a half-day, by mid-afternoon we found ourselves whizzing along the M4. Now, various events made this a lovely long weekend in Pembrokeshire: choccy Easter eggs on our place settings on the Sunday, visiting the monks on Caldey Island and even a walk barefoot on the beach on the Saturday made for a perfect weekend with my beloved. Even a contretemps with a gent in a Vauxhall Cavalier, who drove into us at a petrol station, couldn't spoil it. But one event stands out and probably will forever. On arrival on the Thursday evening we decided to go for a drink in what looked like the nicer of the two pubs in the village. It was too. Nice exposed oak beams, a roaring log fire, horse brasses on the wall and everything looking like it had lived there through two world wars. In fact, some of the furniture looked like it had been through a third. This was what we were after, though – the perfect place to unwind. We noticed that they had a restaurant upstairs, and reading through the menu we decided to come for a meal on one of the evenings over Easter. The restaurant was in darkness due to the late hour, but after we'd spoken to the barmaid she happily took our names and booked us a table for two on the Sunday night.

"Did you want to buy some raf-fle tick-ets as well?" she asked in a gloriously melodic singy-songy Welsh accent, "cos we be 'avin' a bit of a raf-fle 'ere on Sunday night, see, eight o'clock, an' you won't want to be missin' for that."

We declined the offer, but thanked her anyway and whiled away the rest of the evening staring into the flames of the log fire until closing time.

Sunday came and we were looking forward to our meal, so wearing our Easter Sunday best bib and tucker we set off for the quarter-mile walk to the pub. Walking along the lane, all was quiet apart from a murmur in the distance that grew increasingly loud as we approached the pub. Going through the door was an achievement in itself. Never in my life, before or since, have I seen so many people crammed into a country village pub. We weren't exactly wearing outfits that would look out of place at The Palladium, but we were a tad overdressed, though to be honest I don't think anybody noticed or even paid any attention. A lot of pushing and shoving, use of the elbows and an occasional "Excuse me" got us to the bar. The barmaid from Thursday served us.

"What be you 'avin', me lovelies?" she asked.

Shouting, I said that we hadn't come for a drink and that we had a table booked.

"Not tonight, you 'aven't, love-ly." The blank look on my face prompted her to give further explanation: "The restaurant is closed tonight on account of it being Easter Sunday, see."

No, I didn't see. I confirmed that we had booked the table on the Thursday evening, and pointed in the general direction of the noticeboard where she'd written our names and pinned them to it.

She wandered over and found the note.

"Oh yes, you're right, love-ly," she said. "Oh well, nev-er mind, we can do you a bask-et of chips or some-thing if you like."

What choice was there? It was already half past seven and we weren't likely to get something to eat anywhere else. She produced a bar menu – everything with chips or chips with everything, the choice was ours. Two jumbo sausages and chips were ordered, yes in a 'bask-et', and now the next challenge arose: somewhere to sit. Before that could happen a swaying gent appeared clutching a book of raffle tickets and a beer mug containing several notes and a fair smattering of coins.

"You wanna buy some tick-ets? Raf-fle is at eight, you see. Not got long now," he said, rattling the beer mug and waving the book of tickets two inches from my nose.

In for a penny, as they say. With £5 of tickets purchased, the quest for a seat was recommenced. There weren't any. One table, though, looked a possibility. This giant of a man was sitting there with his tiny wife sitting on the opposite side alongside their toddler son. The wife had nothing to amuse herself apart from the vision of her husband supping his pint in front of her.

The son was also drinkless, but was amusing himself with the beer mats, flinging them across the table at his father and shouting, "Pee-yow, pee-yow, pee-yow!" as he did so.

The father put his pint down mid-table.

You know that moment when you can see something is about to happen, but the people that it's going to happen to can't? Well, this was one of those moments.

The very next "Pee-yow!" sent two-thirds of a pint of lager sailing and cascading through the air, coating the table and the floor and soaking Dad. The three of them stood up instantly, as if the Queen had entered the room, and the mopping-up procedure immediately got under way. While this was still in progress, thanks to the bar staff and half a dozen bar towels, the three of them slipped quietly out the door. So, with everything dry again and them gone, the opportunity was seized and we nabbed the table.

Another round of drinks was got in before the sausage and chips turned up and the anointed hour of eight o'clock came and went. No sign of any raffle. More drinks – nine o'clock. No sign of any raffle. In fact, it was getting up towards ten when the landlord finally appeared clutching a clipboard and a bucket, which was over half full of neatly folded-in-half raffle tickets. A space was made for him on the table about six feet from us and everything was almost ready for the grand draw.

"Let's 'ave a bit o' hush, then," he called out, and the noise level dropped to a muttering. "OK, 'ere we go, then, for the raffle. 'ave you all got ya tick-ets at the rea-dy?"

Unless you were there you would not believe the suspense and tension. You know that moment when Dennis Taylor lined up the final black in the 1985 snooker final? Well, it was greater than that.

"Get on with it, I-vor," shouted a voice at the back.

"I'm do-ing it, I'm do-ing it," protested Ivor as he thrust his hand into the bucket, momentarily catching his hand on the handle and almost sending the entire contents onto the still-sticky lager-decorated floor. "Here we go then: num-ber sev-en."

He held the small green piece of paper up in the air like Neville Chamberlain in 1938, while running his eyes down the list that he had on his clipboard. No answer came from the two million people now squeezed into this pub. Suddenly he found the name on the list.

"I've got it – Pat... Bailey." Why the pause in her name, I don't know, but that's how he said it.

Desultory clapping followed and a couple of shouts of "Well done, Pat" were heard.

I got the drinks in – yes, again. This was going to be a long night. There were fifty prizes in this raffle.

"Num-ber elev-en," shouted Ivor.

No answer, and another reference to the clipboard was needed.

"Pat... Bailey," he said after a few seconds.

Less clapping and only one "Well done, Pat" this time.

Perhaps everybody else was trying to work out the odds of having your name drawn out of the hat, or bucket, twice in a row. The best bit was Pat wasn't even in the pub; she'd gone to the Canaries for Easter and here she was two prizes to the good already.

Ivor carried on unperturbed. "Num-ber six-teen."

Everybody held their breath.

"That's me!" cried a voice from the back, and he came forward to collect his prize, a £1.99 cheapo bottle of plonk from the local convenience store, two doors down.

Ivor thrust the bucket in my direction to draw out the next ticket. He looked at it and checked the clipboard again.

"Pat... Bailey."

It couldn't be, three out of four – not possible. Ivor was getting hoarse now shouting over the noise which had returned, so he called out to a member of the bar staff to fetch him a drink: "Alice."

You know the famous song by Smokie, 'Living Next Door to Alice'? Well, you know the other equally well-known version? It was this version that my girlfriend decided to quote from at that moment in a loud voice, but with the racket only I would have been able to hear her. However, in the microsecond she quoted it, the volume dropped at the same moment. I looked at her in disbelief. She looked back, eyes staring and hand clamped firmly over her mouth. We both looked round tentatively. No one had heard her say it, unbelievably.

I volunteered her to get the drinks in as a penance, and I was put in charge of our raffle tickets. Ivor was now getting anyone within a ten-foot radius to draw out the tickets, including a couple of lads that were sitting behind him, and also near us, who up until this time had minded their own business.

Sure enough the cry came, "Pat... Bailey."

The next ticket was drawn.

"Pat... Bailey."

I could stand it no longer. "You're having a laugh!" I exclaimed.

"Oh no," said Ivor. "She's gone and bought over fif-ty quid's worth of tick-ets, you know."

Finally, somewhere around half-eleven the raffle finished, though you wouldn't have known it as Pat Bailey's myriad of prizes, ranging from chocolate Easter eggs of various different sizes to bottles of wine and baskets of flowers still adorned the far end of the bar. She even won the giant fluffy yellow chick that had been hanging from the ceiling for the previous two months in expectation of this very night.

We were reliably informed by a local that "We didn't want to be win-ning that; it's been up there all this time and I bet it don't 'arf stink."

This, of course, was before the 'no smoking in pubs' law came into force.

With the raffle over, a few people melted away into the night and we were starting to flag a bit too. Ivor turned his attention to the two lads.

"How you do-ing, Tom?" he asked.

Tom muttered something about he was fine and introduced Ivor to the other lad. "This is my mate from uni. He's just come down for a few days to stay with me over the Easter break."

"Got a name, 'ave you?" asked Ivor.

"Yeah, it's Sean."

"Thought I hadn't seen you round 'ere afore," said Ivor. "Do you sing at all?"

"No, no, I don't," said Sean.

"Aw, go on. 'Ave a song, why don't you? Do a Tom Jones, cos they like a bit of Tom Jones round 'ere, you know."

Sean, not surprisingly, turned down Ivor's most gracious offer, although this didn't prevent Ivor from reeling off a list of

Tom Jones songs from memory as if he was reading a concert playlist.

My girlfriend and I looked at each other and we were both wearing 'I've had enough now' looks on our faces. We stood up to go.

"You're not go-ing, are you?" exclaimed Ivor in disbelief that we should want to be anywhere else.

"Yes, it's past our bedtime," I claimed. "Thank you for a memorable night," I added. Although he nodded he did look slightly bemused as to why I should have said that, so I gave him a bit more: "Oh, and thanks for the entertainment – wonderful."

Smiling this time, he said, "That's quite OK," and momentarily turned back towards Tom and Sean. Then swinging round, he called out, " 'Ere – what en-ter-tain-ment? 'Ere!"

But it was too late, we'd gone. Looking back, I gave him a smile and we were out the door and closing it and a great memorable evening behind us. An evening that has left me with a permanent subconscious reaction to any raffle. Whenever I'm at a raffle and the first ticket is about to be drawn, only two words spring to mind: Pat... Bailey.

I Blame Victoria Pendleton!

It had been quite a successful day at the races. Well, to be honest it hadn't been – that is, until the last race, when my horse romped home and the whole day (with a little bit over) had been paid for at a stroke.

The drive home is always going to be slow whatever time you leave, and today was no exception as a few thousand racegoers clogged the surrounding roads.

Just before the car came to a complete halt in the traffic queue, we nearly had an accident. A woman, probably in her late-fifties/early-sixties, on her pushbike slewed right across the road in front of us, causing us to brake very sharply. This woman had absolutely no control whatsoever of her bicycle, and I was somehow prevented from winding the window down and issuing forth suggestions, such as "Why don't you get a bus pass?" or telling her she was an idiotic farm animal – one that produces milk and moos!

After finally overtaking her, we caught up with all the traffic at the junction, and there we sat for the next ten minutes or so.

With such a long wait, it was inevitable she would catch us up. Sure enough, after a minute or two I could discern in the wing mirror this figure squeezing herself and her pushbike between all the cars and the very narrow grass verge. She squeezed past us, and I was again prevented from making a comment or offering her some advice!

The grass verge narrowed even more as it reached the junction, but still she carried on as if her life depended upon it. As she reached the next car but one in front of us, she nearly lost her balance. If she had, she and the bike would have toppled into the four-foot-deep ditch which was lying in wait on the other side of the verge. But no, she managed to scramble past. This time, no comment was required!

With one foot on the ground, she finally wrestled the bike around the junction and into a small car park, which contained three cars and a builder's lorry.

She opened the hatchback of a small silver Peugeot, folded the bike up and put it into the back of the car. She wasn't done yet, though – she then proceeded to warm down!

The next two minutes we were subjected to a multitude of warming-down exercises, including bending left and right with arms akimbo, stretching in all directions, toe touching and star jumping. She was still going at it when we finally reached the junction and turned right, leaving her to her post-pedalling workout. I don't know why she couldn't have just used her car and joined a gym!

I ask you, was it really that much of a rush to warm down, and to risk her life with a pushbike in heavy traffic just to get back to her car? I blame Victoria Pendleton and all our other great Olympic cyclists. There's people out there who ten years ago would never have dreamt of riding a bike, and now we have a myriad of accidents just looking for somewhere to happen!

Can You Get a Lonely Planet Guide for It?

(Overheard Conversation in a Fish-and-Chip Shop)

So there I was minding my own business (for a change, I hear you say) in this fish-and-chip shop. I had already placed my order, so was standing, hands in pockets, waiting for the chips to fry when two lads of student age came in.

"Cod 'n' chips twice, please, love," said the slightly taller one.

"We're just waiting for chips" came back love's reply.

The two of them moved back from the counter, and the three of us now stood in a chip-waiting companionable silence, though not for long.

The slightly shorter one was first to speak: "Where's Veg-e-tar?" he asked the taller one.

"What?" asked the taller one, looking puzzled.

"Where's Veg-e-tar?" asked the shorter one for a second time.

"It's a James Cameron film, innit?" replied the taller one helpfully.

There was a slight pause now as the short one considered this possibility.

I heard him mumble, "*Avatar,*" before suddenly exclaiming, "Veg-e-tar!" out loud again for the third time, before adding, "Is it one of those new African countries, like South Sudan?"

"What are you on about? In fact, what are you on?" asked his taller mate.

By now, me and him as well as love and the chap chip frying were curious and ready for the answer to one or other, or indeed both questions.

"Well, everywhere you go, takeaways or restaurants, they serve food from this particular country. I've never not seen it advertised," said the shorter one firmly.

"I've never heard of the place," said the taller one, before adding, "anyway, they don't in here."

"They do, look!" said the shorter one, pointing at the boards listing all the chip-shop delights on the wall behind the counter.

"It's there, look – Veg-e-tar-ian spring roll," the shorter one added indignantly.

The taller one looked at his mate with an air of embarrassment and despair.

"Vegetarian, not Veg-e-tar-ian! It's for vegetarians, innit?" said the taller one, while having a sneaky look round to make sure that no one else had overheard the conversation.

But he was too late – we all had.

"Yeah, that's what I'm saying. I didn't realise there were so many living here and that they have their own menu!" said the shorter one in all seriousness.

"You've lost the plot, mate!" said the taller one. "You really have!"

"Why have I?" asked the shorter one, but he didn't receive an answer.

By now the chips were cooked and I was served my requested large portion!

As I headed out the door I heard the shorter one say, "I wonder if you can get a Lonely Planet guide for it?"

I'm sure I heard the taller one's reply. It isn't repeatable and I'm thinking you can probably guess what it was, or at least something like it!

I Hope You Haven't Wasted It

It had been quite a warm day for so early in the year, and, having arrived home, the temperature drop was very noticeable in the common passageway which divides one property from another. It is usually quite dark, as there are only two windows in the whole passageway which let in any light at all, and the sun didn't usually stream through either of them until late in the afternoon.

I only had to walk past one of the windows, and shot a glance out of it as I did so. As I reached my door, I heard a strange sound from further down the passage.

"Zzzzt!" it went.

I ignored it at first and continued fumbling with my keys.

"Zzzzt!" it went for a second time.

It was no good – curiosity had got the better of me and further investigation was required.

As I rounded the corner, there in front of me on the other window was what could only be described as an infestation! There must have been at least fifty flies covering the window.

OK, we're not talking biblical plague proportions here – that really would be an exaggeration – but bad enough just the same.

I dashed back to my door and literally flew through it. My mother had been expecting me, and clearly not the whirling dervish that did burst in.

"Have we got any fly spray?" I blurted out.

I have to be honest: the response to this question from my mother was not the one I was expecting.

"Why, what are you going to use it for?" she puzzlingly asked.

"What do you think I'm going to use it for?" came back my bewildered reply.

She muttered something about the cupboard under the sink, and ten seconds later I set off down the passageway shaking the can of fly spray.

It worked too! After about three minutes of first of all constant spraying, followed by sporadic spraying to 'bayonet the wounded', as it were, I'd managed to rid the whole window and passageway of the entire fly population (what a hero!) and returned to my door with a real sense of triumph!

As I walked back in the door, the second equally puzzling question was asked: "I hope you haven't wasted it?" enquired my mother without looking up.

So no triumphal return, then, no brass bands playing, no victory procession march through the town to celebrate my coming back from the front. Nothing!

"Well, what have you been doing with it?" became the third puzzling question.

"Killing flies, obviously," I replied, a little disheartened my killing spree hadn't been better recognised, and fearing any chance of receiving a medal for gallantry had somehow passed me by.

"Well, I just hope you haven't wasted it, that's all," she said in final conclusion.

"It's a can of fly spray. I mean, what else are we keeping it for? It's hardly a decoration or an ornament, now, is it?" It was all I could think of to say in my final crestfallen defence.

Within two minutes the can of fly spray was returned to the cupboard under the sink, and a dustpan and brush taken out to sweep up the bodies.

Despite my lack of a Victoria Cross, I could see where she was coming from. The expression 'I hope you haven't wasted it' can be attributed to a lot of items that once had to be used sparingly, and I'm sure it is a very common expression used by any survivor of the Blitz. Bless her, x.

By Kind Permission from BEAULIEU MOTOR MUSEUM

The Nightmare of Casterbridge

A long weekend in Dorset was planned and had been booked for months. It was decided that Dorchester (the Casterbridge of Thomas Hardy fame) was to be the base, and day trips out to the surrounding towns, beaches and countryside were to be made from there.

The plan was to go on a Thursday to avoid the usual mad Friday rush, and to not come back until the following Monday. As it was early September and the kids had gone back to school after the summer holidays, it was just going to be a few days of unrushed peace and quiet away from it all. And that's exactly what it was. We saw all the things we wanted to see, did all the things we wanted to do, and went to all the places we wanted to go. A perfect little long weekend away.

However, the journey down to Dorset from Kent by train on the previous Thursday was something else! For what in reality is not the most difficult of journeys turned into an absolute nightmare from start to finish! Who said, 'It's better to travel hopefully than to arrive'? I can assure you, oh no it isn't!

It started the second we arrived at our home station – there were no trains.

Apparently the engineering works which had been operating throughout the Wednesday night and into early Thursday morning were seriously overrunning, and were likely to continue to do so for the next hour or two. So to get around the problem buses had been laid on to take all impending passengers several stations up the line to where all the trains were terminating and departing from.

"Next bus will be about ten minutes!" shouted out a railway employee.

The ten minutes came and went.

After about twenty minutes or so a bus drew up outside the station. Now, I'm not saying this bus was old, but I swear it was steam-driven, had solid tyres and had 'By Kind Permission from Beaulieu Motor Museum' written on the side of it. It creaked and shuddered to a halt in front of the station, and us dozen or so passengers piled in and found an old horsehair-stuffed seat to sit on.

Off we trundled at around twenty miles an hour, calling at all stations. "Is this as fast as it goes?" shouted out an annoyed passenger, but no answer was heard in return, and he carried on complaining to all those around him.

When we arrived at the station where all the trains were starting from, the train was standing at the platform ready for us, although not actually going anywhere for half an hour as it had only just arrived with a down service!

Finally we were off – but not for long. Less than an hour later we arrived at another station, where our train just stood for ten minutes at platform three. Then came the all-important announcement over the station Tannoy: "The train at platform three will be terminated here, as it is running late!"

It was a new one on me – I had never heard that excuse before. As it had been the fast train into London, and there were no more stops, frustration ruled. Some passengers who had passed the disgruntled stage, and were already at the very annoyed stage, were now nearing the seriously apoplectic stage.

To avoid the fast-approaching riot, a spokeswoman tried the calming tactic of saying the next fast service would be half an hour; or passengers could catch the slow train, calling at all the minor stations along the way. Working on the theory that as long as you are moving you were moving rather than standing there becalmed, we decided on the 'stopper' and duly jumped on when it arrived at the station.

A 'stopper' it was too. Every small station was stopped at, and each time for several minutes, but finally the train rumbled into London Victoria. We had arrived, at least an hour and a half later than we should have done.

The journey across London was taken by taxi in an attempt to 'speed things up a bit', to quote my comment, but a demonstration near the Houses of Parliament soon put paid to that particular plan.

'Save the Environment!' said one banner. 'Stop the Pollution!' said another, which kind of defeated the object as we were all stuck in traffic with engines idling.

After a ten-minute taxi journey, which had taken nearer twenty-five, we arrived at Waterloo. I paid the taxi driver, and we walked onto the station concourse, and guess what? You're quite right – we had just missed the train by about thirty seconds. The next one would be in half an hour.

Sure enough, half an hour later the train was pulling out of the station on its way to sunny Dorset. But not for long! Three miles into the journey we stopped. Up ahead of us somebody had been seen running along the railway lines with a gun in his hand, and the ordinary police, the British Transport Police, the dog handlers, the helicopters and a firearms team were now on hand to sort it out. Apparently it had been going on since early morning. Something about this chap coming home early and finding his soon-to-be-ex-wife and friend together, and an act of defenestration followed. The quote I heard later on was "It was a domestic and the chap had lost it!"

Now, you would think there wasn't much else that could go wrong. We were on our way again and with each passing minute we neared our final destination. In fact, I thought I would actually try and grab a quick snooze, and had just nodded off when:

"Tickets please!" bellowed out from the guard, or conductor or ticket inspector or whatever name they call them nowadays.

I fumbled in my pocket and produced my somewhat creased ticket and waited while he made his way down the carriage towards me. He was a rather portly gentleman and the narrow confines of the aisle necessitated a kind of swaying motion, first to the right, then to the left, as he squeezed between the seats checking all the tickets as he went.

"Tickets please!" he bellowed out a second time just as he arrived at my seat.

I handed my ticket over to him and he stared at it momentarily. As he was in the act of handing it back to me, he paused and looked at it again.

"Where did you get this?" he asked a little sternly.

I was tempted to say, "On special offer at the Co-op," but by the look he had on his face he didn't seem to be in the mood for my sardonic hilarity. "At the station. I told the bloke at the ticket office what I wanted – travelling today, coming back on Monday – and that's what he sold me," I explained.

"It's s'wrong ticket, innit!" came back the reply.

"I don't know – is it?" I replied.

"Yeah, come 'ere – I'll sort it owt for ya. Huh, typical amateurs for ya, innit!"

He proceeded to spend the next five minutes fiddling with all the controls and buttons on his ticket machine, while all the time making a decidedly odd concoction of muttering and murmuring noises, seemingly directed towards ticket-office staff and their abilities to do anything right. Finally he pushed a button and his machine sprang into life. A ticket churned out, stopping just a few inches from the end of my nose.

"There ya go, mate – that's the one ya want. Ya good to go nah!" he stated firmly, while at the same time swishing his hand through the air and whipping the ticket along its perforations off the machine.

The ticket he gave me looked exactly the same as the one I had previously, but as long as it got me to where I was going to, and back again, it didn't really matter, especially as in less than an hour I would be there.

Some hope!

I attempted another snooze, but could feel the train starting to slow, and it finally came to a complete halt in the middle of nowhere. The only signs of life were some scrawny-looking sheep, who were obviously used to trains whizzing by at 100 miles an hour, so they eyed the one stopped in front of them with some suspicion. It didn't stop them from chewing, though.

It took at least ten minutes before we found out what was going on, when the public address system first crackled and then announced, "Sorry for the delay. There's been an incident up ahead, and we're currently fourth in a stack, so we could be 'ere for a while!" It was the now familiar voice of my portly ticket seller.

We were there for a while too – the best part of an hour!

At one point the ticket seller walked through the train, and a chap several seats in front of me literally stopped him in his tracks (pun intended!) before asking, "How much longer are we gonna have to just sit here?"

"I dunno, mate – it varies. I fink there's been a suicide and it depends on 'ow bad it is, don't it?" came the ticket seller's rather unhelpful reply, before adding, " 'Appens all the time on this line, mate. Ya lucky to git a day when it don't 'appen!"

When we eventually did start moving again it was at a regulation twenty miles an hour, and after a few miles we trundled through the next station at the same speed. The platforms were deserted of passengers and only contained station staff and emergency crews attending to the 'incident', which seemed to be two black bags on platform one. I won't go into details – I will leave it to your imagination.

Amazingly this was the last event of the whole nightmare, and the rest of the journey passed by quite normally!

When we finally arrived at Dorchester we were nearly four hours later than we should have been and it was getting dark, so a quick look around the shops was out of the question as they were all shut!

Did have a nice time while down there, though.

If I'm honest I can find a positive. At least all the events happened in just the one journey and were not spread out over several train trips in the course of a fortnight!

A WEIRD AND WONDERFUL HISTORY
OF JOB INTERVIEWS
PART THREE

All Hours God Sends

I was working as a temp and a fixed short-term contract had just come to an end when quite by chance an opportunity arose for a job paying me a not dissimilar wage to my previous full-time post, so I just had to put in for it.

It was a full-time permanent job in the admin department of a large firm only a short train ride away from where I lived, and I was pleased when they rang to offer me an interview only two days after I had sent them my CV.

It was a lovely spring day as the train rattled along. The daffodils were looking lovely growing on the railway embankments, lambs were gambolling in the fields and the oilseed rape was coming into full bloom – it was a lovely spring day!

After alighting at the station and walking past a few houses and shops, I found myself walking along a country lane with fields on both sides. In the distance I could see what looked to be a huge warehouse. 'Reckon that's it!' I thought.

Arriving at the warehouse, an equally huge 'RECEPTION' sign greeted me. 'Reckon it's in here!' I thought.

Once through the glass doors I was into the foyer, which was so large you could have held a wedding reception for one hundred guests in it! What made it seem even larger was the tiny lady sitting behind the reception desk.

She asked, "Can I help?" even before I managed to get to her!

"Mr Jenkins. I'm here for an interview," I confidently replied.

She looked down at her desk and shuffled a few papers about before finding the one she was looking for.

"Oh yes. Take a seat and I'll let them know you're here," she stated firmly while crossing my name off her list. I didn't have long to wait before my interviewer turned up and shook me vigorously by the hand.

The interview went well. He had my CV in front of him and I answered all his questions about where I had worked before and what experience I had gained. He then started chatting about Formula One as he caught me looking at the large picture of Jackie Stewart winning at Monaco on the wall behind him, and launched into a tirade about the previous weekend's Grand Prix.

Everything about the interview was going fine until the question of hours of employment came up. Now, I was used to working in an office from 9 a.m. to 5.30 p.m. Monday to Friday, and this job was working in an office, so naturally I assumed the hours would be roughly the same. I couldn't have been more wrong!

"Oh, I've not told you the hours of employment, have I?" he stated in a matter-of-fact kind of voice. Before I could answer, he told me: "The hours of employment are 7.30 a.m. to 6.30 p.m. with half an hour for lunch Monday to Friday, and every other Saturday from 7.30 a.m. to 6.30 p.m. with half an hour for lunch, and one Sunday in four from 8 a.m. to 4 p.m., but no lunch, unfortunately, as the canteen's shut on Sundays. Oh, and you also receive ten days' [only] annual leave, and you won't have to make the time up if you need to go to the doctor or dentist. Does all that, and those hours, suit you?"

He looked up at me. He should have looked down really, because my face was on the floor! I burbled something asking whether the one Sunday in four was on the same weekend as the Saturday I would be working, and he confirmed it would!

The interview came to an end not long after that, and he walked me all the way down the stairs, finally shaking hands in reception before I walked shell-shocked through the glass doors, almost literally.

Walking slowly back to the train station, I started doing the maths!

"No wonder the money's almost the same!" I exclaimed out loud.

Looking back towards the warehouse, I hadn't noticed until that moment that there were no windows in the whole building.

"I wouldn't see daylight for days on end!" I exclaimed even louder. "That's not a job; that's moving in!" I exclaimed out loud for a third time.

A few days later I received a letter from their personnel department (shows how long ago this was) thanking me for attending the interview, and they were pleased to offer me the post of administration assistant.

Initially I had no choice but to accept, but fortunately on the Friday afternoon, before I was due to start on the Monday morning, I received a phone call from my agency offering me a new fixed-term contract with 'normal' office hours!

I telephoned the warehouse's personnel department to tell them I wasn't coming. They were a bit miffed, to say the least – I think in part because they thought they had at last found someone who wanted to take root in their admin department!

Musical Chairs and the Super Soup Slurper

This next experience took place in a restaurant. "Not again!" I hear you say. I actually don't know why it is I seem to have endless 'experiences' in restaurants, but I can honestly say I went past the 'Why me?' stage years ago.

The events below happened in a hotel restaurant somewhere on the south coast over a period of a few days, several years ago.

This probably quite recently retired couple arrived in the hotel restaurant at around eight o'clock, by which time those who had arrived at seven thirty, when it had opened, were just about to tuck into their starter, yours truly included. We all had a table allocated to our room, and theirs was towards one corner with a sea view; but oh no, they didn't want to sit there!

"Oh, we like to sit side by side," said Mrs Wife.

The tables were all in such a position that this would mean moving four other tables to accommodate them, three of which were occupied, and I'm guessing you've already worked out who was sitting at one of them! So there I was right in the middle of my loaded-potato-skins starter, standing up, holding my plate while three waiters, two waitresses and the maître d' shifted the tables through various angles, just so this couple could sit side by side as if sitting together like passengers on a bus.

Job done, we all sat back down again.

"No, not quite right, is it, dear?" said Mr Husband.

Mrs Wife didn't answer. They stood up and moved their table a few inches to the west and sat back down. She then whispered something quietly across the table and they both stood up again and changed seats. Seconds later their allocated waitress arrived with the wine list. After a quick perusal of the list, Mrs Wife leaned across the table and they both stood up and changed seats again!

For his starter, Mr Husband decided on 'today's special' – tomato soup – and it duly arrived piping hot.

Mrs Wife had decided she didn't want a starter, but commented, "That's all right, Derek – you go ahead. You know how much you like your soup!"

Derek did go ahead too! Having scooped a spoonful from the bowl, he held the spoon momentarily before leaning into it for his first mouthful.

"Sch-lurppp!" went Derek, and the first spoonful was gone.

He sat back briefly as the spoon went in for round two. Again it appeared full to the brim and was held suspended in mid-air as Derek leaned into it for his second mouthful.

"Sch-lurppp!" went Derek, several decibels louder than the first time, and on it went. In fact, twelve full spoon-loads and twelve sch-lurppps were heard, with each sch-lurppp marginally louder than the previous one.

Their main courses and desserts in contrast were eaten in complete silence, but only if you discount the endless moaning between courses and comments such as "What meat did they say this is?" and "Are your potatoes as hard as mine?" and

"Hasn't it got a funny taste?" and "It's not like the one we had in Brighton."

The next night, the waiting staff were ready for them, their table and chairs in position. They arrived at exactly the same time, sat down and didn't move again.

"Have you any more of that delicious tomato soup?" enquired Derek.

"We do, yes," replied their allocated waitress (though not the same one as the previous evening, I might add).

"Can I have that for my starter, then, please?" asked Derek.

You know what's coming next, don't you? Aha! Well, you'd be wrong! As the previous evening, having scooped a spoonful from the bowl, he held the spoon momentarily before leaning into it for his first mouthful. Just as his lips reached the spoon, the hearing aid in his left ear, which I had previously failed to notice, sprang into life.

"Pweeeeeee!" It went off like a kind of mini foghorn. However, no slurp! Again, he sat back briefly before going for the next mouthful. As he lent in, "Pweeeeeee!" Off it went again. Twelve spoonfuls, and twelve pweeeeeees were heard before he finally finished.

Mrs Wife still went without a starter and, compared with the previous evening, the rest of their dinner was eaten in comparative silence.

On arrival in the restaurant on the third and last night, I noticed their table had been set for four, and sure enough just after eight o'clock they arrived, but this time with a younger couple in tow. From comments made, they were clearly the couple's son and daughter-in-law, and they all took their seats at the table, each couple sitting side by side.

"I can recommend the tomato soup," said Derek loudly.

"Yuck!" replied the son, and buried himself in the menu.

"Perhaps there's none left," suggested Mrs Wife.

"There had better be," replied Derek indignantly, before adding, "been looking forward to it all day!"

Their allocated waitress (third night, third different waitress, I might add) arrived to take their order. During the ordering it transpired the waitress had come from Hungary, though not on that particular day, I'm guessing!

"Oh, have you!" exclaimed the son before launching into an instant memory, which he shared with us all. "Oh yes, I've been to Hungary. I loved it, especially the potatoes[!] and the goulash. Oh yes, and I absolutely loved everything about Prague!"

And before you ask, no, no one corrected him.

No prizes for guessing Derek had the tomato soup. As before, he scooped a spoonful from the bowl and held the spoon for a second or two before leaning into it for his first mouthful.

As his lips reached the spoon, "Pweeeeeee!" Off went his hearing aid. He took his first mouthful. "Sch-lurppp!" as he devoured the first spoonful. He sat back briefly, and went for it again. "Pweeeeeee! Sch-lurppp!" Wait for it. Go again. "Pweeeeeee! Sch-lurppp!" Twelve spoonfuls and twelve pweeeeeee sch-lurppps. And as on the first night each sch-lurppp was a tad louder than the previous one.

Mrs Wife, the son and daughter-in-law sat in an embarrassed silence throughout, and, after the starters were finished, Derek proceeded to tell them all about the main courses and desserts he and Mrs Wife had eaten on the preceding two nights.

They were leaving the next day, and on going down to dinner that evening I noticed on the 'Specials Board' tomato soup was notably absent!

Life Is Not a Re-Hearse-al

What once started out as a joke has now become an obsession, and I think somebody somewhere is trying to tell me something.

We all at some time in our lives have been involved in a funeral, and equally we have probably all at some time seen a funeral procession go past on its way to the crematorium or boneyard.

During the first forty-five years of my life I had seen several go past me, and always used to tip my hat (in the days when I wore one), or at least give some kind of acknowledgement towards the departed in their flower-bedecked coffin, as the hearse trundled along just above walking pace. Probably the one I remember the most was a Gypsy funeral many years ago near Orpington in Kent. It took nearly half an hour for all the horse-drawn vehicles to go past!

Nevertheless the sightings of any kind of funeral were few and far between, and not something you saw every day, or every week – or even probably every month, for that matter. So, how is it, then, that about three years ago all of the following began.

A funeral came up behind me as I was walking along. I duly raised one hand in a slight wave/salute gesture, and it went past. The very next day the same thing happened, the difference being I was walking in the opposite direction, with the hearse heading the same way, and very clearly coming *from* a funeral as the back was empty!

"That's the second hearse I've seen this week, and it's still only Wednesday!" I thought out loud.

Just two days later, on Friday morning it happened again. A loaded hearse, covered in a myriad of flowers, with at least two other funeral cars and several ordinary cars, drove past me at regulation speed. Mid-afternoon on the same day I ran into the whole shebang coming back again! That made four hearse sightings in as many days!

It was not as though it was winter either, when a small town's aging population tends to drop off the perch with more regularity. This was late spring going into summer and the weather had been nice and warm for a couple of weeks.

To be honest I had forgotten all about my hearse-spotting by the following Tuesday, so when a funeral drove past me I did a double take.

"Not again!" I exclaimed out loud, and louder than the previous Wednesday.

Two days later I witnessed two funerals on the same day, in two different towns, twenty miles apart. This was getting silly. By now, I reasoned, I had seen more funerals in ten days than in the whole of the rest of my life. And no, it doesn't end there either. Rarely does a week go by when I fail to witness at least one sighting of a hearse either going to or coming back from a funeral. Not just in my home town either; everywhere I go, there they are, waiting for me. I sometimes wonder if I shouldn't become a professional mourner and pallbearer!

It's actually quite unbelievable and a tad unnerving. Does anyone have any theories? I suppose there is one consolation: I have only witnessed these funerals and not been the subject of one, unless perhaps it was in another life!

Dancing in the Aisles

A new supermarket opened near me.

Not one of those huge just-outside-of-the-city types, just a small express type.

One thing I've noticed about express supermarkets is that they tend to have all the items in the right aisle. In a large out-of-town place to make a cup of coffee you have to walk miles, as a jar of coffee is in one aisle, the sugar in another and the milk twelve aisles and a two-minute walk away! Then if you want toast with your coffee, you need to buy the butter in aisle two and the bread in aisle twenty-two!

Of course large supermarkets usually have large trolleys and large aisles with people who seem to want to spend all day and half the night in them, whereas express supermarkets are exactly the opposite. Their narrow aisles tend to force you to make a mad dash round them with (or without) a basket.

There is one other little problem, though. It stems from the fact that they do have the bread and the sugar and the coffee in the same aisle; and as most of the patrons buy at least one of

74

these commodities, there is a fair chance you will witness the basket dance.

Punter number one is walking north to south; punter number two, south to north. They clearly see each other, but there is no eye contact. Punter number one steps to their left; punter number two steps to their right. Pause. Punter number one takes a large stride to their right; punter number two takes a large stride to their left. Pause. Punter number one takes an even larger stride to their left; punter number two takes an even larger stride to their right. Their baskets momentarily touch! There may be a slightly embarrassed "Ha ha ha!" There may be a, "Ya dancin'?" / "Ya askin'?" interchange, but mostly not a word of conversation passes between them. The whole manoeuvre is completed when somebody takes charge and dives around the outside of their opponent.

I can honestly say this has happened to me, or at the very least been witnessed by me every time I have visited the express store. They open early, they close late, and it happens in every aisle, though here is a tip for you all. If you want to witness the express store do-si-do, try the bread aisle. It never fails!

What? Now?

It was while on a weekend trip to Aldershot in Hampshire that probably without doubt the most bizarre response to a frequently asked question was overheard.

While walking nonchalantly in the main pedestrian shopping precinct, which wasn't particularly busy considering it was Friday afternoon, I quite by chance looked up at the opportune moment.

About twenty yards in front of me was a couple, probably in their mid-to-late forties, walking along with four bags of shopping between them, the wife walking the regulation one and a half paces behind her husband. Clearly they had done their weekend shop early and were on their way home with the goodies.

Between me and them was a chap walking along minding his own business (unlike me), with his hands buried deep in his jacket pockets.

The husband was slightly unbalanced by the weight of his two shopping bags, which caused him to lurch slightly further to his right than planned. This actually caused the chap in front of me to move slightly to his left to avoid being careered into.

It was at this point the husband asked the question. "Excuse me, do you happen to have the right time?" he said, crossing his hands and carrier bags over so he could use his right index finger to first point at his left wrist and then tap it several times.

"Not an unreasonable request," I hear you say. I mean, it's probably something we have all asked someone at some point in our lives. However, the response from this chap was partially astounding and definitely weird.

"What? Now?" came his reply in a somewhat loud and angry voice.

The husband (as well as myself) looked at him for a second in disbelief! Was he serious? I mean, when asked the question how did he normally respond?

"I can't tell you now, but meet me back here in an hour and I'll tell you then!" or "I'll give you a time and you decide whether it's right or not!" or "I can tell you what it was a week ago last Tuesday!" or even "I'll be able to tell you at midnight on New Year's Eve!"

Although frozen in suspended animated disbelief, the husband still managed to stammer, "Erm, yes please."

Removing his mobile phone from his left jacket pocket and flicking it on, we at last had the long-awaited answer to one of the world's most simple questions.

"Three thirty, mate, all right?" finally came the chap's reply, and he walked on.

"Yes. Thank you" came back the husband's response as he looked towards his wife for clarification of what had just happened.

He tried looking for it from me too, but somehow when he looked round I'd gone!

Dewdrop and Daisy

A long weekend stay was booked in Weston-super-Mare. It was a first for me as I previously hadn't even visited the town, let alone stayed there, and I was quite looking forward to it. A day trip to the island of Steep Holm offshore was planned for one of the days, but a very strong easterly wind and some blustery showers soon put paid to that and so it meant being marooned in Weston for the day. But that's another story.

If you have been reading this book from the beginning and not just dipping into it here and there, you will have noticed how it always seems to happen to me when it comes to restaurants. Well, in that case I have no choice but to recount the wonderful tale of the retired couple staying at my hotel, and the complete and utter inanity of the conversations which took place over their breakfasts and dinners.

I feel I should tell you right from the off I never actually did know their names, but their nicknames were acquired by the fact that Dewdrop always had one on the end of his nose (and it always seemed to be on the point of dropping off at any moment) and his wife Daisy was so named as she was always wearing a top or a dress with large daisies printed all over it. She even wore a daisy fascinator at one point!

They had every one of their meals sitting near the window so that whenever the conversation dropped one or both of them would peer out of it.

I hadn't noticed them at all, to be honest, on the first evening until halfway through their main course, when Daisy suddenly shouted out at the top of her voice, "Look, a seal, a seal! I can see a seal!" she exclaimed, while going quite red in the face as she began to enter the first stages of hyperventilation, although she wasn't stopping there. "Look, can't you see it? It's over there. I can see a seal, and it's red and pink!"

A large proportion of the sitting diners initially hadn't looked up from their dinners, but they did now, and peered over in Dewdrop and Daisy's general direction.

"Red and pink? Are you quite sure, darling?" asked Dewdrop quietly across the table, aware most of the eyes of Somerset were upon them at that moment.

Oh yes, she was certain, and nothing was going to sway her belief in what she was looking at.

Hearing all the commotion, from out of nowhere the restaurant manager arrived to witness this peculiar sighting from his hotel, and to perhaps contact the BBC to tell them to send David Attenborough. Peering out of the window and showing absolutely no signs of emotion, he said, "I think you'll find, madam, that's a marker buoy bobbing up and down with the tide," before adding, "seals aren't usually that colour, in my experience."

I don't think she was convinced, but accepted his explanation all the same, and spent the rest of the meal on seal watch!

This was the highlight of their first dinner, and from

murmurings around me it seemed to be the highlight of most of the other diners' dinners too.

The next day dawned rather grey and a bit rainy, and when they came down for breakfast they were discussing "Where can we go that doesn't entail us getting wet?" They were still discussing it when the waitress arrived. The breakfast menus had been sitting on the tables, and up until that moment they had only given them a momentary glance.

"Good morning. I will take your order in a moment, but in the meantime would you like tea or coffee?" asked the waitress chirpily.

"Oh, a large pot of tea for both of us, please," answered Dewdrop.

Daisy nodded in agreement, and proceeded to peer out of the window as they waited for their waitress to return with their Asian infusion.

A few moments later, she returned with a large metal tray containing a milk jug and two large pots of tea. She put them down on the table and produced her notepad from out of her pocket all in the same movement.

"What can I get for you today, then?" she asked.

"Full English breakfast for me, please, with scrambled egg," requested Dewdrop.

"Can I just have a plate of in-between bacon, please," asked Daisy firmly.

The waitress stood holding the pencil above her notepad for a few seconds in suspended animation, before looking at Daisy with the same quizzical expression the rest of us in the immediate vicinity were wearing.

"I'm sorry – can you say that again, please?" asked the confused waitress.

"In-between bacon," said Daisy, a tad annoyed she'd been asked a second time.

"I'm really sorry about this, but I don't know what that is. Can you explain it to me, please," asked the waitress.

Daisy took a deep breath. "Well, there's bacon, isn't there? Sometimes you have it crispy and sometimes you have it soft. I don't want it crispy and I don't want it soft. I would much prefer it somewhere in between," explained Daisy.

"Oh, I see, I think," replied the waitress, and scribbled something down on her notepad, before adding, "and what else would you like?"

"No, nothing else – just the plate of in-between bacon, please, especially as I have to go into hospital next week with my knee," confirmed Daisy.

The waitress looked at her, not with a confused expression this time, more of one of complete and utter disbelief, as did the rest of the diners. What her knee had to do with anything we shall never ever know.

The waitress almost ran to the sanctuary of the kitchen with the order, before returning several minutes later with a 'full English' and a plate of in-between bacon!

"Perfect!" said Daisy as she chomped her way through several large rashers.

By the time I arrived for dinner that evening, Dewdrop and Daisy had theirs well under way. It was only seven thirty, so they must have started early, and all was quiet too.

They seemed quite happy munching away until suddenly, "Waiter! Waiter!" cried out Dewdrop at the top of his voice, loud enough so the whole restaurant looked round.

The waiter duly arrived, looking extremely concerned. "Is everything all right with your meals, sir?" he asked.

"Oh yes, of course," replied Dewdrop.

Daisy nodded and continued eating.

"It's just that geography has never really been my strong point – in fact, you could say I was hopeless at it. Could you tell us where we are, please?"

The waiter was now wearing the same complete-and-utter-disbelief expression as the waitress had worn at breakfast, but managed to stammer out the answer: "Er, erm, Weston-super-Mare, sir."

"Oh yes, of course. Thank you very much," replied Dewdrop, and promptly went back to eating his dinner, but not before wiping the end of his nose.

Daisy's turn! "Is that Weston over there?" she asked, while at the same time pointing out of the window in the direction of the town.

"Yes," replied the waiter.

"Well, what about that over there? Is that still Weston?" asked Daisy, moving her extended arm only a few inches to the right and still pointing out of the window.

"Yes," replied the waiter.

"Oh, so it's all Weston!" exclaimed Daisy, a huge sense of relief in her voice.

"Yes," replied the waiter for a third time.

He then gradually edged away from their table, hoping they wouldn't notice his absence. They didn't!

Breakfast next morning and the fun continued. Dewdrop and Daisy walked into the restaurant at eight thirty-five, and the same waitress walked slowly over to their table. In fact, she couldn't have walked any slower if she had been going to her execution.

"Good morning, Ellie, and how are you today?" asked Dewdrop cheerfully, clearly now on first-name terms with all the staff.

"I'm very well, thank you," replied Ellie. She added, "What can I get for you both today?"

"I'm sorry we're a bit later than usual today," said Daisy. "We've been up since five past seven, and it takes me fifteen to twenty minutes to get my face on," she added, without explaining what had happened to the other hour and fifteen minutes.

A full English breakfast and a plate of in-between bacon was duly ordered for a second day running. Today's twist to proceedings was they ordered coffee and not tea. After several failed attempts at pouring it out Daisy gave up, and Dewdrop had to take over and do the honours.

At dinner that evening they had the same geographically aware waiter!

"And a very good evening to you, Dario. And how are you today?" asked Dewdrop with the same cheerfulness he had shown at breakfast.

Dario was fine, to begin with, but seemed more than a little startled when he was called upon to adjudge whether a boat on the water was actually moving or not!

My last sighting of Dewdrop and Daisy was the following morning. They were slightly earlier than usual, but the day began the same.

"Good morning to you, Ellie. And how are you today?" asked Dewdrop in his now familiar cheery manner.

However, before Ellie could open her mouth to answer, "I would like eggs today – not in-between bacon, just eggs!" pronounced Daisy.

"Oh," said Ellie, before continuing with, "well, would you like them fried, boiled, poached, scrambled, or we can do you an omelette if you'd like?"

You cannot possibly imagine the size of the trauma this caused. The debate between Daisy and Dewdrop went on for nearly ten minutes on how she wanted her eggs.

At one point Daisy said out loud, "But I only have an apple for my brunch!"

And the debate continued. A final decision was made. It was to be a plate of scrambled eggs – nothing else. No toast, not even a pot of tea or coffee today, just scrambled eggs.

Ellie arrived back around ten minutes later with the most massive portion of scrambled eggs you've ever seen in your life, and Daisy set about tackling it as if her life depended upon it. In fact, she only stopped eating the once to ask Dewdrop, "How far is it approximately to where we're going today?"

"About forty minutes," replied Dewdrop while wiping the end of his nose.

"That's OK, then," replied Daisy, and returned to her scrambled-egg mountain.

I'm guessing they left the hotel later that morning, and went on to the next part of their holiday, as I never saw them again.

However, on checking out of the hotel myself the following morning, the receptionist happened to notice my home town on the original booking form.

"Oh, we've had another couple from there staying here this week. They checked out yesterday. Did you know them?" she asked, looking at me for a response.

Needless to say she didn't get one, and I very quickly changed the subject.

Snoring In St Albans

With the help of a very nice lady from the St Albans Tourist Information Centre, a lovely little bed and breakfast in a 1930s semi-detached house was found on the outskirts of the city.

After a whistle-stop tour of the surrounding area and the city itself, the bed and breakfast I'd booked for the night was finally tracked down.

I was met at the door by the owner, a short round lady with dark hair, probably in her early sixties, and shown the room. Perfect – just what was required for the one night. There was only one other person staying in the house – a youngish chap who seemed to be a rep for a pharmaceutical company.

After freshening up, it was decided dinner was to be had at the local Italian restaurant. Arriving back at the house, the whole place seemed to be in darkness although the time had only just gone ten o'clock. This necessitated a very slow creep up the stairs with my shoes in my right hand.

At the top, immediately in front of me was the communal bathroom. I made this my first stop, as the bottle and a half of rosé I'd had with my dinner had started to take effect. Walking through the bathroom door I could not believe what I saw. I have to be honest, I have never seen anything else quite like it in my entire life!

There standing in front of me was virtually the entire European toilet-roll mountain! At least twenty per cent of her bathroom was stacked high with them. And not just stacked either. Every shelf, window sill and cupboard was full of them. Two even stood on the side of the bath! A fresh one hung from the toilet-roll holder, and it even had a spare standing by the side of it on a little shelf seemingly put there specifically for the purpose! Two loaded toilet-roll dollies even stood on the left and right of a window sill, with two more toilet rolls between them!

"But was it a quiet night's sleep?" I hear you ask.

It was – well, until about two o'clock in the morning, that is.

I was awoken by the most peculiar sound. It is almost impossible to describe, but there was a similarity to a jet fighter with the throttle cutting in and out, a bit like you hear at an air show. But an air show and a B & B in St Albans at two o'clock in the morning couldn't be much further apart, could they? The noise was coming from the landlady's bedroom. Now, don't get me wrong – I've heard snoring and I've heard snoring, but this was something else. I swear even the pictures on the walls of the landing were rattling!

Amazingly, somehow I managed to get back to sleep using a combination of duvet and pillows over both ears – that is until five o'clock in the morning. Exactly at five o'clock in the morning – at precisely that time – I was awoken by at least two people shouting their lungs out downstairs. Once fully awake, I decided to investigate. It wasn't anybody shouting; it was just people talking loudly and was coming from the owner's private sitting room. Listening at the door, I quickly realised it was coming from the television set, which had clearly been left on at full volume!

I went back to bed and, astonishingly, for a second time went back to sleep, using the duvet-and-pillows trick again, only to be awoken for a third time just after six thirty by the young rep chap leaving for his first appointment.

At breakfast, the landlady was questioned about her television set.

"Oh yes, sorry about that. It does that sometimes – just automatically switches itself on at five o'clock in the morning. I don't know why it does it – just always seems to," she said unsympathetically, not noticing the bags under my eyes.

'No, clearly you don't know why it does it!' I thought.

Thankfully I was only booked in for the one night, and have never been back to either the bed and breakfast or, indeed, St Albans.

I've stayed at lots of other places, though, but you have to ask yourself, to B & B, or not to B & B: that is the question!

Drunk in Charge of an Interviewee

I had sent my CV to a firm in Dover. They were looking for someone with experience rather than qualifications and the hours and salary definitely suited, so why not? Nothing ventured and all that.

Within a week a letter had arrived requesting I attend an interview. The company was a small building firm, but the address for their office and indeed the interview seemed to be in a residential street.

Deciding to allow myself plenty of time to find the place, I arrived in Dover before one o'clock for my interview at two. Just as well really as it was a tad difficult to find. I had been right – it was a residential street. The buildings were all old and three or four storeys high and had either been converted into flats or, in some cases offices. Having found the address, I looked up the several stone steps at the glass-panelled white front door. On the wall to the right was a metal plaque with the name of the firm in decaying black letters written on it.

"Good – found it!" I said to myself in a low whisper.

As it was only one thirty, I decided on a walk round the block and arrived back just before one fifty-five.

I walked up the steps and pushed the door. It didn't open. I tried again. The door was definitely locked. To the left of the door were six doorbells, but no clue as to which one I was after! I decided to play Russian roulette with them, and pressed the one I logically believed it would be. I listened carefully, but there was no ringing sound coming from within, and no one appeared on the wide staircase I could see through the glass.

Considering it was lunchtime, it was a little eerie there was virtually no one about, either in the street on foot or driving past, and the time was now ticking on.

I tried again, this time pressing all six doorbells one after the other. Still no answer. I tried knocking on the door – loudly. Still no answer!

The time was now well gone two o'clock. I walked backwards down the steps and was on the verge of giving up when I shot a glance up the road.

Coming towards me, staggering and at times wheeling, was a man in his late forties with unkempt curly greying hair. He was wearing a brown sports jacket complete with leather patches and beige trousers. When I say beige, that appeared to be the colour they had been when he had them new!

He looked suspiciously at me. As I was now at the last-resort stage, I decided to go for it.

"Hello. I'm looking for…"

I didn't get any further. "Mishter (hic) Jenkinshh, is it?" he slurred.

"Er, er, yes, that's right. I'm here for an interview," I stammered, momentarily overcome with the overwhelming smell of beer fumes.

"Shorry I'm a bit late (hic), but I bin at lunsch," he explained while fumbling in his pocket for the keys.

I'm guessing he'd been to the pub. In fact, there was irrefutable evidence that I was right!

After finding the right key – on the fourth attempt, I might add – we were in the front door. He then wobbled from side to side in front of me up four flights of stairs, with me thinking, 'Any minute now he's going to fall backwards!' Somehow, though, he didn't, and we went through a door on the second floor which led into an outer office.

"That would be your deshk," he slurred while pointing at a crumbling table that looked as though it had been fire-and-water damaged during the Blitz.

Taking me through another door, we were now in his office. As he made his way around to the other side of the desk he bumped his leg on the corner, winced and promptly bumped it a second time on the other corner. He winced again, and sat down.

"Take a sheat," he proffered.

'On exactly what?' I thought. There wasn't a 'sheat' to be had anywhere!

"Oh, shorry – ya gonna 'afta git one (hic) from the uvva offish," he suggested.

A chair which had equally survived the German Luftwaffe stood in the outer office. I fetched it and made myself as comfortable as possible.

The next thirty minutes or so were taken up with my interview. All these years later I don't remember anything particular about the interview – but at least it was about twenty years ago. He wouldn't have remembered anything about me twenty minutes after I had left the office!

A 'Dear John' letter duly arrived in the post several days

later. I actually considered phoning to ask him for some feedback, but I don't think there would have been much of a point really, do you?

Momentous Occasions

Being born in the mid-sixties, I managed to miss some of this country's and indeed some of the world's most momentous occasions. I missed the Great Train Robbery, I missed John F. Kennedy's assassination, I missed Christine Keeler and the Profumo Scandal, and I missed John Lennon asking everyone else to rattle their jewellery. I even managed to miss Winston Churchill's funeral and the trial of the Moors Murderers.

However, there were two events of the 1960s, in which, although I wasn't actually there, I did still manage to play an active part!

My mother was heavily pregnant on that famous Saturday afternoon when England and West Germany (as was) walked out onto the hallowed turf of Wembley Stadium. It was 30 July 1966 and England were in the World Cup final for the first (and most likely last) time.

Now, it's not for me to go into details of the game. Every inch of the game has been analysed a million times over. The Goal That Never Was, "There's some people running onto the pitch…", Nobby Stiles dancing with the trophy, etc., etc. No, my part in the proceedings involves the fact that with only a minute to go and the game seemingly won, and having not moved for the best part of two hours, and with the pressure of an exceedingly large lump pressing down on her bladder, my mother was absolutely bursting! But what did it matter? The referee was about to blow the whistle, and there would soon be relief (literally) all round!

The Germans had a free kick. Wolfgang Weber scored. It was 2–2. Extra time!

"Well, I'm not moving now!" stated my mother in a loud voice.

Nor did she. She managed to stay long enough to see Geoff Hurst hit the ball, and it flying into the back of the net, as the most famous piece of Kenneth Wolstenholme's commentary concluded with "…it is now!"

Then she had to go (literally). But don't worry, she was back in plenty of time to see the Queen handing the trophy over to Bobby Moore.

We'd won – the most famous moment in our footballing history – and I'd missed that as well, by just three and a half weeks.

OK, so I may not have been there in spirit, or even there cheering them on, but you have to admit I was there in part, and according to my mother certainly made my presence felt!

So now we're into the late sixties. However, I was obviously too young to remember the tragic deaths of Donald Campbell and Jim Clark, the Summer of Love and Sgt. Pepper. I missed the assassinations of Martin Luther King and Bobby Kennedy, and John & Yoko in bed. Also, I have no recollections of man landing on the moon – or have I? Did I not play an active part in this too?

Apollo 11 took off on 16th July 1969 and four days later, on the 20th, the world sat around agog at their television sets waiting for the first man to set foot on the moon. Just like everyone else, my family sat waiting (and waiting) for this, probably the greatest moment in our history!

Finally the moment had come. Neil Armstrong began to slowly descend the steps of the *Eagle* spacecraft. Just as his foot came off the ladder and hung in (I was going to say mid-air, but that wouldn't be quite right, would it?) the moon's atmosphere, he began the utterance of those famous words.

"It's one small step for man…"

I was promptly sick!

Luckily, from previous experience my mother knew the first signs of one of my impending 'barfings', and she managed to bundle me in the direction of our fireplace. Obviously there was no fire burning, it being mid-July, and I successfully filled the grate!

By the time me and the fire grate were mopped up, the moment had passed and everyone had missed this momentous occasion, Buzz Aldrin having joined Neil on the moon and they were busy bouncing around. We've all seen the famous footage a dozen times, but it's not really the same as saying I saw it live, is it?

So, you have to admit, I did play my part in two of the most famous events of the decade. The seventies were quite bland by comparison – that is if you exclude the unfortunate incident during the Queen's silver jubilee celebrations, but that's another story for another day!

You're Making This Up, Aren't You?

It was our anniversary. Two whole years since our first date together had to be commemorated, so gradually over a period of ten days or so a plan was formed to celebrate the occasion. Nothing elaborate, nothing out of the ordinary, just a nice quiet simple idea, a relaxing day out, dinner in the evening and stay over. What could go wrong? Well, just about everything you could imagine!

The day started with a drive to Samphire Hoe. For those of you who are not in the know, Samphire Hoe is situated between Dover and Folkestone in Kent. It was created from the spoil removed when the Channel Tunnel was built, and has become in itself a small country park. However, today was not really the day to be visiting. The sky was overcast and it was very cold, made even worse by the biting east wind coming straight in off the sea.

In fact, after only a short walk we were back in the car with the radio on. It was while I was constantly changing the channel, trying to find something half decent to listen to, that it happened. All of a sudden… nothing! The radio went off and so did all the lights on the dashboard. A reset and a turn of the key in the ignition produced an extremely sick noise from the engine. Tried again, and again, and again, but it was no use – the thing was dead!

A phone call to the AA followed, but you try explaining where you are when where you are doesn't actually appear on most maps – that is, until only quite recently.

They managed to work it out in the end, though, and they were 'on their way'. In the meantime, music had been restored with the aid of the iPad, and we now had David Soul singing "Don't give up on us, baby" coming from the speakers.

As he sang the line "We're still worth one more try", I said in a loud voice, "Go on, do like the man says: give it one more try!"

A turn of the key in the ignition and the whole car started. The lights beamed out from the dashboard, the headlamps came on and the radio crackled back into life, which gave us a combined cacophony of David Soul harmonising with the Sex Pistols singing 'Pretty Vacant'!

Once Johnny Rotten was turned down, a further phone call to the AA was made to cancel the previous one – but as they hadn't even left, there was no harm done.

Having been at Samphire Hoe for well over an hour and a half, it was time to move on. We were booked in for dinner and an overnight stay at the place we had shared our first date. The table was booked for seven thirty, and as we had arrived a lot later than intended there was just enough time to change and freshen up before going downstairs to the restaurant.

Our waitress arrived within minutes with the menus and wine list. The wine choice was fairly easy and a bottle of rosé was requested. The food choices took a little longer; but once ordered, I poured us a second glass and we sat back and waited for our starter. And waited, and waited, and waited! If it had been somewhere else we would probably have stood up and walked out, but as the place is fairly remote and we weren't in a rush anyway, as we were staying the night, it seemed a tad churlish to complain.

I suddenly saw our waitress coming towards us, a plate of food in each hand. I was going to try and attract her attention, but there was no need to – she'd arrived.

"Who ordered the lamb?" she asked cheerfully.

"Er, that would be me," I replied, before adding, "although it would be nice if we could have our starters first!"

I swear her face went pure white.

"Tell me you've had them," she stammered, and we both shook our heads.

"I'm really sorry. I don't know what's happened, but I will go and sort it out right now!" she replied – and sounded quite angry too, I might add.

Within minutes, she was back.

"I'm really sorry about this, but who ordered the baked Camembert for their starter – it's just we haven't any left!"

"Can you bring us both the menus back and we'll start again," I replied. The waitress did as she was asked and we started again. She took the order and vanished into the kitchens. Within two minutes she was back.

Having noticed our, by now, nearly empty bottle of wine, she came with a question. "Would you like another bottle of the Zinfandel, on the house?" she beamed.

Now, it doesn't take much for me to be easily bought; and as it was going to be free, gratis and for nothing, I could hardly be impolite and say no, now, could I? The waitress disappeared off again and it was almost ten minutes before she came back.

"Erm, it would, erm, appear you ordered the last bottle. Can we get you something else?" she said sheepishly, and I swear she grew even whiter.

Now, you could either shout and scream at this point or start to laugh, and I could feel myself doing the latter, but somehow managed to keep a straight face.

"We'll have the first bottle of rosé you can put your hands on," I replied.

A second bottle was delivered to our table, and our starters arrived moments behind it. Perfect – nothing else could go wrong! Wrong!

During the eating of our starter, the waitress arrived back.

"You did order the lamb, didn't you?" she asked.

I nodded.

"I'm sorry – there's none left!" she replied.

"You're making this up, aren't you?" I responded with a slight smile.

She shook her head.

"But I've already seen it once!" I added.

"Yes, that was the last one. I'm really sorry – can I get you something else?" she asked in a very quiet voice. The poor cow was almost in tears!

"I'll tell you what," I said: "I'll have the chicken-and-leek pie."

Her eyes lit up. "We've got that, I know we have!" And off she dashed.

Before our 'mains' turned up, though, there was yet another twist. The young couple to the side of us seemed a little nervous – I think they were probably out on their first date. Another waitress arrived with their main course.

"Who's having the lamb?" she asked.

The girl raised her left hand slightly, and was duly served.

After the waitress had gone, I just had to ask, "Excuse me, where did you get that?"

"I ordered it," she responded.

"Yeah, so did I – didn't get very far, though," I replied.

With the time now approaching ten o'clock and with the main courses finally served and eaten, there was just enough time for pudding! Our waitress arrived with the menus for a third time, and a banoffee pie and an apple crumble with custard were ordered. Off she went, but not for long.

"Would you mind having the apple crumble with cream as we've run out of custard?" She said it so quietly you could barely hear her. She looked so distraught.

I stood up and put my arms around her – it was just an instant reaction.

"I've never had a night like this, ever!" she said, sniffing back tears.

The apple crumble duly arrived, but actually with ice cream, so even that didn't turn up right!

At around ten thirty, and having sat there for just over three hours, she finally arrived with the bill. It was for around sixty pounds, but she had completely crossed through the total at the bottom.

"Call it forty quid!" she stated quite firmly, before adding, "You're not paying a penny more!"

I gave her the forty quid – well, I wasn't going to argue – before slipping an extra £5 note into her hand. After all, it wasn't her fault, and the service had been exceptional. And so our three-hour second-anniversary dinner had finally come to an end.

We went to the same restaurant for our third-anniversary lunch, but this time a pint and a bowl of cheesy chips did the job just as well!

Watching the World

Jeff Jenkins

www.ingramcontent.com/pod-product-compliance
Lightning Source LLC
Chambersburg PA
CBHW051842040426
42447CB00006B/655